"Dr. Pennington is a true acade[...] [...] him. Frankly, you'd have a hard [...] [...]ing so, as he is exactly the kind of pastor-theologian we need more of. Just the mention of 'philosophy' conjures images of classrooms I lack the will to inhabit, but in his engaging and accessible style Pennington invites ordinary learners to sit at the feet of the most extraordinary philosopher. Jesus the Philosopher is concerned not merely with our dying and eternal state but with our living—and with our abundant living, at that. You hold a book that will expand your vision for human flourishing, as you gaze through ancient lenses on the face of the Savior."

—**Jen Wilkin**, author and Bible teacher

"I wish I had been introduced to *Jesus the Great Philosopher* much earlier in life. It would have saved me from much struggle and error. I wish I had had a book like this one to teach how we can see and understand the way in which the truths taught by the world's greatest thinkers are reflected in many ways in the everyday world around us—yet find their ultimate source and end only in Jesus. Deep and wide, informative and accessible, challenging and humane—this is a book that will help you not only to think better but to live better too."

—**Karen Swallow Prior**, author of *On Reading Well: Finding the Good Life through Great Books* and *Fierce Convictions: The Extraordinary Life of Hannah More—Poet, Reformer, Abolitionist*

"When many people think of philosophy, they think of arid and abstract syllogisms. That's not this book. This book, written by one of the most brilliant biblical scholars of this generation, makes a compelling case for Jesus as Lord, as Savior, and as Philosopher. This philosophy of Jesus is incarnational rather than abstract, holistic rather than syllogistic, and revelatory rather than just argumentative. This book addresses the mind, the heart, the soul, and the life. That's why it's the book we need right now. Read and find wisdom. Read and find Christ."

—**Russell Moore**, president, The Ethics & Religious Liberty Commission of the Southern Baptist Convention

"Our world continues to struggle with who we are, what we are about, and where to find happiness. *Jesus the Great Philosopher* addresses these issues and answers these problems by presenting Jesus as our all in all. Jonathan Pennington's research and writing are a true gift to the church. Throughout this book, you will find his curiosity infectious and his excitement contagious. With the uncovering of ancient truths and the discovery of ageless practices, you will be motivated to love Jesus for all he is—the beginning and the end, the philosopher for all of life. Enjoy this book and learn to live with Jesus as your great philosopher."

—**Kyle Idleman**, bestselling author of *Not a Fan*, *Grace Is Greater*, and *Don't Give Up*

"In *Jesus the Great Philosopher*, Jonathan Pennington lifts up an often-neglected aspect of Jesus's identity in order to showcase the beauty of Christianity as a way of life—an answer to the meaninglessness and confusion felt by many today who look for solutions in philosophies that bring no lasting satisfaction. Pennington gives us a Jesus-directed introduction to many of life's most profound questions."

—**Trevin Wax**, senior vice president of theology and communications, LifeWay Christian Resources; author of *Rethink Your Self: The Power of Looking Up before Looking In* and *This Is Our Time: Everyday Myths in Light of the Gospel*

JESUS
THE GREAT
PHILOSOPHER

JESUS
THE GREAT
PHILOSOPHER

Rediscovering the Wisdom
Needed for the Good Life

JONATHAN T.
PENNINGTON

BrazosPress
a division of Baker Publishing Group
Grand Rapids, Michigan

© 2020 by Jonathan T. Pennington

Published by Brazos Press
a division of Baker Publishing Group
PO Box 6287, Grand Rapids, MI 49516-6287
www.brazospress.com

Printed in the United States of America

Library of Congress Cataloging-in-Publication Data
Names: Pennington, Jonathan T., author.
Title: Jesus the great philosopher : rediscovering the wisdom needed for the good life / Jonathan T. Pennington.
Description: Grand Rapids, Michigan : Brazos Press, a division of Baker Publishing Group, 2020.
Identifiers: LCCN 2020019058 | ISBN 9781587434655 (paperback) | ISBN 9781587435140 (casebound)
Subjects: LCSH: Jesus Christ—Teachings. | Wisdom.
Classification: LCC BT306 .P395 2020 | DDC 230—dc23
LC record available at https://lccn.loc.gov/2020019058

The author is represented by the literary agency of The Gates Group.

21   22   23   24   25   26   7   6   5   4   3   2

In keeping with biblical principl
creation stewardship, Baker Pu
ing Group advocates the respor
use of our natural resources.
member of the Green Press I
tive, our company uses rec
paper when possible. The text
of this book is composed in p
post-consumer waste.

green
press
INITIATIVE

To Ben, Dave, Justin, Michael, and Scott
of the I&C writing group.

This book came into being only through the encouragement,
challenge, and joie de vivre of our fortnightly gatherings.
Thank you for doing life together so beautifully!

"You do not want to leave too, do you?" Jesus asked the Twelve.

Simon Peter answered him, "Lord, to whom shall we go? You have the words of eternal life."

John 6:67–68

Contents

YOUR
PERSONAL
LORD AND
PHILOSOPHER

Philosophers, Martyrs, and Canoes

Imagine a Christian church today somewhere in the American Bible Belt, a place where Christianity has roots deep enough and branches wide enough that worshipers have built a mega-church. This church accommodates thousands in multiple services every weekend. Picture the bustle and vibrancy of such a place, with its modern, clean, and comfortable architecture, including built-in coffee shop.

Now look up at the walls as you enter the sanctuary. You can see beautiful banners that remind churchgoers of precious truths about the One they are here to worship, Jesus. These large, deep-blue and gold, hand-sewn hangings each proclaim a name or description of the Lord drawn from the Bible. Your eyes scan across the many names, each of which communicates something important—Shepherd, King, Savior, Messiah, Friend of sinners, Immanuel.

And Philosopher.

Philosopher? Not likely. What would your reaction be? Is the preacher going to conclude with an altar call inviting you to "pray to receive Jesus as your personal philosopher"?

Now let's mentally time travel to another church service. Let's visit the gathering of a group of pious Christians some eighteen hundred years earlier, in the ancient city of Dura-Europos. This fortress town in modern-day Syria sat right on the Euphrates River, a formidable stronghold.[1] It was ruled by a succession of people including the Parthians and Romans. Dura-Europos was remarkably diverse in culture, language, and religion, with places of worship for Christians, Jews, and various Greek and Roman cults—a truly metropolitan place to live and raise a family and plant gardens and worship one's god.

That is, before it was attacked and overrun in AD 256. While the city was besieged, the inhabitants realized that the only way to protect the city was to cram everything they could find into the houses and shops that were built into the fortress wall—every bit of trash, debris, and rubble they could get their hands on. This worked for a while, but eventually the city fell to the Sasanians. The attackers came in, killed the inhabitants, took what they could find, and then completely abandoned the place. The desert sands began to drift and blow over the skeletons and drinking cups, eventually covering it over completely.

It wasn't until right after World War I that European archaeologists stumbled upon Dura-Europos. When they did, they found that the buildings that were built into the side of the walls were an archaeologist's dream! They were completely intact, preserved, and untouched because of the stuffed debris. Among other important discoveries, the researchers found a house church, frozen in time.

Now we can look at their church walls. What were their decorations? Like those in our imagined megachurch, these faithful Christians also used their walls to remind worshipers of who Jesus is. The painted images in this ancient church depict Jesus in various ways, as the Good Shepherd, the Great Physician, and the Water Walker. And as a Philosopher. In fact, in all the pictures of Jesus healing, teaching, and performing miracles, he is wearing the telltale philosopher's robes, has the haircut

Yale University Art Gallery

Figure 1. Wall painting from Dura-Europos of Jesus healing the paralytic

that indicated his status as a philosopher, and is standing in the posture of a philosophy teacher (see fig. 1).

Philosopher. Painted on the walls of the church. Why?

○ ○ ○ ○

It turns out the Dura-Europos believers were not alone. By the year AD 100, to everyone's surprise, Christianity was spreading far and wide throughout the mighty Roman Empire. Around that time a man named Justin was born in Flavia Neapolis in Palestine, about thirty miles north of Jerusalem. As a thoughtful and sincere young man, Justin began to search for life, for some direction that would give him wisdom and meaning. He tried to be a disciple of a Stoic teacher, the most popular philosophy of the day. Unsatisfied, he tried connecting himself with a Peripatetic, a teacher of the ways of Aristotle. This too proved unworkable. When he approached a Pythagorean philosopher, he was told that he did not have the required training in music, astronomy, and geometry. Next, he began training in the ways of Platonism, with hopes that he would find the truth and behold the god of the Ideals.

He finally felt like his pursuit of wisdom was going well. But the true God had other plans. While walking near the sea, Justin fell into intense dialogue with an old man, a man who turned out to be a follower of Jesus of Nazareth. The man thoughtfully engaged Justin, challenging him with several insightful questions, pushing him to think about the soul and humanity's fate—our fate that depends on the true and eternal God. Justin asked how he could learn to practice this philosophy. The old Christian's answer was that it is the Hebrew prophets, inspired by the Spirit, who are the true philosophers of the world, and who point to the true wisdom to be found in Jesus. Justin's heart was set ablaze, and he began reading and meditating on the prophets and the "friends of Christ," coming to love the truth they spoke.

All of this is described autobiographically by Justin in what became his very famous book *Dialogue with Trypho*. This book was written in the classical dialogue style (first made famous by Socrates and Plato), where the teaching mode is an intense conversation. *Dialogue* comes from sometime in the 150s or 160s, after Justin had moved to Rome and set up a Christian philosophy/discipleship school.

This autobiographical info from Justin has a purpose. *Dialogue* tells the story of a Jewish man named Trypho who approached Justin and started a conversation with him. Why? Because he recognized by Justin's apparel that he was a philosopher. Even as spurs and a ten-gallon hat would communicate "cowboy" to us, Justin's robes, haircut, and manner said "philosopher." Justin explains to Trypho his own story—how he came through many insufficient philosophies to finally find the true philosophy of Jesus. The Old Testament prophets were philosophers. Jesus was the greatest philosopher. And now as a disciple of Jesus, Justin is a philosopher too. Philosophy is a way of finding true life, Justin explains, and now he has found this true life in Jesus. Christianity is the true philosophy that through faith and the power of the Spirit enables people to see the world in a certain way and to live accordingly. It is the way to the truly Good Life.

And so this is what Justin did. Living in Rome, at the heart of the empire and its many philosophical schools, he taught people the true philosophy of Christianity. He dialogued, defended, apologized (that is, gave reason for his faith), both in person and in writings like the *Dialogue* and his *First Apology* and *Second Apology*.

And it got him into trouble. Justin was eventually arrested and tried before the city prefect Rusticus, one of the teachers of the great Stoic emperor Marcus Aurelius (and no fan of Christians). Because Justin refused to sacrifice to the gods and show obeisance to the emperor, he was executed. Up until then he was known as Justin the Philosopher. After his execution for his faith, he became known as Justin the Martyr. Justin's martyrdom is the appropriate consummation of his life following the philosophy of Jesus. Jesus the Savior-Philosopher died faithful to God. So did his faithful disciple, Justin the Philosopher-now-Martyr.[2]

○ ○ ○ ○

Fast-forward to another dialogue that happened some years later, in AD 1999. The location is not Rome but Iowa, at the Republican Party primary debate in the run-up to the 2000 presidential election. The moderator of the debate asked each candidate this question: "What political philosopher or thinker do you most identify with and why?" The first to answer was then-governor George W. Bush. Without hesitation, in his sincere Texan drawl, Bush answered that the philosopher who most influenced him was "Christ."

Now some might debate how appropriate or erudite of an answer this was, but this is what the future president offered. Bush further explained what he meant, and what he says is more Bible Belt than Beltway and more revivalist than rigorous. "Jesus as Philosopher" meant for Bush that when someone accepts Jesus as Lord and Savior, this changes their heart and thus their thinking. This is how Jesus is a philosopher. That answer is maybe a bit less sophisticated than Justin's, but it's no less sincere. Both Justin Martyr and Governor Bush recognized in Jesus someone who offers true wisdom for how to live well.

When we examine the long space of Christian history between Bush's and Justin's responses, we find a rich tradition of Christians answering the same way. In statues, altar pieces, sarcophagus carvings, sermons, theological treatises, and popular stories, when standing before emperors and governors, Christians have long talked about Jesus as a philosopher and Christianity as the true philosophy of life. Christianity is not just a set of doctrines but a divine whole-life philosophy worth dying for, if need be.

○○○○

But something has changed. Something has been lost. If we were to conduct a Jimmy Fallon–esque "Word on the Street" interview today, I doubt many, if any, would offer that Christianity is a philosophy and that Jesus is a philosopher. No one is making "Jesus the Philosopher" banners for their church foyers. Amazon offers minimal hits that contain both "Jesus" and "Philosopher" in their titles, and the few that are found are usually academic historical studies, not for the average churchgoer. Syllabi for courses in Bible colleges, university religion departments, and seminaries do not present Jesus as a philosopher. This is not to mention university philosophy courses. If a philosophy professor suggested "Jesus" as one of the subjects to study alongside Aristotle, Kant, and Hume, he or she would likely receive the dual gift of raised eyebrows and a reprimand.

But this reflects a major historical shift. Throughout the vast span of the church's history, Christianity has been understood as a sophisticated philosophy of life with Jesus as the Great Philosopher.

○○○○

So what happened? To answer the question of why the modern church has largely lost this way of speaking of Jesus as the Great Philosopher, we must step back. We'll need to understand the seismic shift that happened to the word "philosophy" over the intervening centuries. We'll tackle this in the following chapter.

But for now, we all know that we *don't* put "Jesus," "Christianity," "philosopher," and "philosophy" in the same sentences or even paragraphs. Who cares? Why does this matter?

I think there are four significant things that have happened to the church as a result of this loss of "philosophy" language:

1. Our Christian faith is often *disconnected* from other aspects of our human lives. Christianity has become merely a religion rather than a philosophy of life.

2. We naturally look to other sources—*alternative gurus*—to give us the wisdom needed to live flourishing lives, to find the Good Life.

3. We have stopped asking a *set of big questions* that Holy Scripture is seeking to answer—questions about how the world really works and how to live in it.

4. We have *limited our witness* to the world.

Let's consider these briefly.

○ ○ ○ ○

Disconnected faith. Whether we intend it or not, our modern lives are often built like a chest of drawers, with distinct compartments for each area. Even as we keep our socks, underwear, exercise clothes, and jeans in different drawers (or at least, most of us do), so too our lives have distinct compartments—health, relationships, money, education, leisure, religion.

Christian people also have a specific drawer for Jesus. For some it is a small, low-placed half drawer that is only opened once a week or maybe twice a month on Sundays. For others—especially pastors and missionaries—the Jesus drawer is big and probably at the top of the cabinet with well-oiled rollers. Most Christians' "Jesus drawers" are somewhere in between.

Figure 2
Chest of drawers

A chest of drawers is a great thing for organizing clothes (and hiding cigars from your spouse), but not for structuring our lives. Humans are organic beings who thrive only when the many parts of our lives are connected together. Our bodies, our minds, our emotions, our habits, our praying, our relationships—all of these are intimately related. They can't be compartmentalized, at least not if we want to thrive. One cannot remove the mitochondria or ribosomes from a simple cell and expect it to function. How much more for the infinitely complex human organism! We cannot treat our lives as if the various parts are unrelated and expect to experience meaningful happiness and the flourishing life that Jesus talks about (John 10:10).

Because of various shifts that have happened in the worlds of both theology and philosophy, most Christians today experience Jesus as part of their "religion" or "faith." But it is not clear to most faithful Christians how this relates to the rest of the "real life" of vocations, vacations, relationships, emotions, and, ultimately, happiness. The way we think and talk about our Christian faith is often an exercise in drawer building, not life creation. Christianity may be a great religion, but how it provides a philosophy of life is not so apparent. As theologian Peter Leithart astutely observes, many Christians are dualists, mistakenly living our lives like a layered cake—with supernatural truths on the top layer of an otherwise natural cake. The "church adds a spiritual dimension to my life but leaves my natural world more or less intact."[3]

○ ○ ○ ○

Alternative gurus. In real life, Nick Offerman, most famous for his Übermensch role as Ron Swanson on NBC's *Parks and Recreation*, is a man's man, fully bearded and equipped with all manner of hardcore man skills. He has reached significant enough fame in American culture today that he has published a memoir full of his homespun wisdom. It is cleverly titled *Paddle Your Own Canoe: One Man's Fundamentals for Delicious Living.*[4]

In Offerman's crude and swaggering style, he presents sixteen chapters that follow his own experiences. Each chapter is subtitled with a pithy proverb: "Eat Red Meat," "How to Be a Man," "Measure Twice, Cut Once," "The Moustache Makes the Magick," and several others that would not make it through the editorial process for any publisher concerned about lewdness and vulgarity (such as mine).

What is the man Offerman offering? He's quite aware that he is giving his readers a philosophy of life, a way of seeing and being in the world that promises happiness, based on his forty-plus years of great success so far. The keys to happiness, according to Nick, are found in living a principled life that includes lots of hard work, lots of sex, lots of pork, and a little bit of luck.

Most people won't completely adopt Offerman's philosophy of life, even if they find him enjoyable as a character and comic. But what his memoir represents is what all humans long for and need—someone to help us figure out how to live well, someone who provides both a model and principles for real life. Offerman is inviting people to follow his example and adopt his attitudes. He's a modern-man philosopher, a woodworking, BBQ-eating guru.

Sitting at assorted coffee shops working on this book, I often ran into friends, church members, and students who would kindly ask what I was working on. So I've tried out several "elevator speech" versions of describing Jesus as a philosopher. After one such account, a particularly thoughtful friend shared how this related to his experience. Despite his strong commitment to the church, his experience of Christianity has indeed been one of needing to find alternative gurus. As he described it, he learned from Bible college and many great preachers the *vertical aspects* of Christianity—who God is and what Jesus has done for us—and this is great. But he hasn't found many teachers or leaders in the church who helped him think about the *horizontal aspects* of what it means to be a Christian—vocation, emotions, politics, and so on—in short, a philosophy of life. So he has found help for that elsewhere, in people like today's famous psychologist-visionary Jordan Peterson. (We'll come back to Peterson later.)

I don't think my friend's experience is uncommon. Because we have lost the image of Jesus as a whole-life philosopher, many faithful Christians find other gurus to help them figure out the questions of daily living. Our modern culture has plenty of philosophers on tap. We have philosophers of finance (Warren Buffett), philosophers of what books we should read to feel empowered (Oprah), philosophers of leadership principles (Ray Dalio), philosophers of productivity (David Allen) and how to get into flow (Mihaly Csikszentmihalyi), philosophers of fashion and chic cool (Heidi Klum), philosophers of creativity (Austin Kleon), and philosophers of getting organized and getting rid of stuff (Marie Kondo). Christians often create their philosophy of life from a hodgepodge of these, often adding in a Christianized version of the same thinkers.

Christians and non-Christians alike benefit from such philosophers. This is not necessarily bad or wrong—we should gladly collect good lumber from any forest we can find as we build the houses of our lives. But it's better to realize that Jesus the Philosopher is doing more than speaking to the religious and spiritual parts of lives—the vertical aspects. He is a guru for all human and horizontal realities too. When we lose the idea that Jesus is a life-philosopher, we are stuck looking to alternative gurus, whether of the Offerman type or not.

○ ○ ○ ○

Loss of questions. In addition to Steve Martin (whom we'll talk about in the next chapter), one of the greatest influences on my young comedic sensibilities was Douglas Adams's five-part trilogy (you read that right) *The Hitchhiker's Guide to the Galaxy.* Woven throughout this romping, irreverent science fiction world is the number 42. This figure is significant because, after the supercomputer named Deep Thought ran its program for 7.5 million years, it determined that the answer to the ultimate question of life is in fact 42. This didn't exactly satisfy the recipients present at the time. Deep Thought pointed out to them that while 42 was in fact the answer, they had never specified what exactly the question was. Subsequently, Deep

Thought then created the Earth as a supercomputer to figure out what the Ultimate Question was (Earth unfortunately was destroyed by the Vogons five minutes before its ten-million-year program completed).

I often think of this funny idea that we might finally have the answer but then forget what the question was. I think it is often true about the Bible. That is, Christians believe in the ultimate authority of what is taught in Scripture—we believe it has the answers—but we don't always remember *to ask the right questions* of what the Bible is teaching. So, with our high view of Scripture in hand, we go to the Bible and ask important questions—religious, vertical questions—and that is good. But because of habits and training, we have stopped asking *another set* of questions—the human, horizontal, philosophical ones.

But this is a loss for us because it turns out that the Bible has strong and sophisticated 42-quality answers to the great human questions, the ones philosophy has always asked. These are questions like, What is the nature of reality? How do we know this? What does it mean to be human? How do we order our relationships and emotions? How do we find true happiness? In the modern world, we have forgotten to ask the Bible these crucial questions. And as a result, we have lost a major part of what Holy Scripture is saying and how it is meant to function in the Christian life.

○ ○ ○ ○

Limited witness. Let's return once more to Nick Offerman's canoe-building advice. Not only is he presenting himself as a guru for how to live, Offerman also has very strong negative opinions about the problems with Christianity and Christians. In some ways the book is an antitestimony to his experience of formerly being a Catholic and then "born-again" Christian up until his first year in college. In the chapter "Hail Mary, Full of

Beans," Offerman describes his upbringing in the "fairy-tale" belief system of Catholicism. Protestant Christianity doesn't fare much better as he describes his evangelical youth group experiences. At length and with a palatable vitriol, Offerman lambasts any Christian who would suggest that the moral teachings of the Bible should ever be used in public for any laws. This is all summed up with his aphorism "Horse Sense > The Bible."

From a psychological perspective, Offerman's violent reaction to Christianity reveals more about whatever personal demons he is seeking to exorcise than any particular insight he purports to have regarding the complex questions of church and state. But he does serve as an example of a real person whose early experience in Christianity disappointed him. It disappointed precisely because it was not large enough to make sense of his whole life. Christianity was *part* of his life but was ultimately discardable. It wasn't presented to him in ways big enough to encompass his clever mind and eager spirit. (Plus he liked smoking weed.) The philosophy-of-life things that stuck and shaped him came from elsewhere. Hard work, diligence, family, friendships—these things he learned *outside the church*, Offerman says.

There is no way to know how much of this was the fault of his priests, his pastors, and his own choices. Who we become and what we believe (big philosophical questions) are the result of innumerable factors. But I think Offerman's experience is not entirely atypical. Modern Christianity has often been practiced and taught in ways that divorce it from the rest of "real life." The result is many churched children become adult "Nones." These people are among that 23 percent of the American population who today answer "None" to the question, "What is your religious affiliation?"[5] I suggest that one factor underneath this shift is the loss of seeing Christianity as a whole-life philosophy and Jesus as the Great Philosopher.

The Genius of Ancient Philosophy

In one of his brilliant 1970s stand-up routines, comedian Steve Martin reflects on his college experience and what he calls "the intellectual thing."[1] He observes that people forget most of what they learn while in school. For example, geology doesn't stick with you, Martin says, because it's all facts and figures. But philosophy is different. When you study philosophy in college, Martin notes, "you remember just enough to screw you up for the rest of your life."[2]

This comment reflects the experience of many of us who took the required Philosophy 101 course at our university. We met Dr. Brown, a shortish sixty-year-old man with disheveled hair, a rumpled, half-untucked shirt, and chalk blurs on his pants. After feverishly filling the board with names of German philosophers and lofty ideas, he challenged the class with questions of a mind-melting nature: "Does this chair exist once we leave this room? How would we know this?" "How do I know that I'm not just deep into an elaborate dream right now?" "Is it right or wrong to steal medicine from a pharmacy to help your wife who is writhing on the floor in pain?" "If you're stranded on the ocean in a lifeboat with a prostitute, a twelve-year-old boy, a priest, and a surgeon, whose life is the most valuable to save? And how do you decide this?"

For Steve Martin there is more depth to his joke than may at first appear. While developing his comedy career, Martin studied philosophy at UCLA. He is not throwing grenades from afar. He experienced philosophy.[3] In his *A Wild and Crazy Guy* routine, he considers the big ethical and religious questions that philosophy raises. At one point Martin observes, "It's so hard to believe in anything anymore. You know what I mean? It's like religion. You can't really take it seriously because it's so mythological and it seems so arbitrary. And then on the other hand, science. You know. It's just pure empiricism and by virtue of its method it excludes metaphysics."

This unexpectedly complicated statement, delivered in Martin's mirthful and clever way, reveals a deep reflection. What he was saying was probably lost on his semidrunken audience (as can be heard from the background heckling). But this comment shows Martin's experience with modern philosophy: It asks big questions, but it doesn't provide any answers. It leaves a person lost, uncertain, ambivalent. You remember just enough to screw you up for the rest of your life.

○ ○ ○ ○

However, this is not the whole story. This life-screwing-up is not what philosophy used to do. This common modern experience of philosophy—as irrelevant at best and destructive at worst—is a radical change from how humans have understood and been affected by philosophy over the last three thousand years. Whether coming from Confucius, Buddha, or the Greek tradition of Socrates, Plato, and Aristotle, philosophy was not seen as a collection of meaningless speculations about whether chairs exist when we leave the room.

On the contrary, *philosophy was the necessary bedrock for individuals and society.* Philosophy in the ancient world was the lodestar, the scaffolding, the guide by which humans could experience true happiness; it was the vision for *life itself.* Philosophy

18

provided the vision for the Good and the goodness of life. This is what education is for, according to Plato—to show people what the Good is so that they can orient their lives to it. This is why the city-state exists, according to Aristotle—to enable people to live a truly Good Life. The effect of philosophy was not to bungle the rest of your life but to provide a way of being in the world that offered true life and flourishing. But philosophy has changed.

○ ○ ○ ○

In modern society what is the most respected and valued profession? Who gets the highest regard and honor, both financially and in social capital? I think in modern Western society the answer is a medical doctor. Have you ever noticed what I call the "scrub factor"? When you see someone wearing medical scrubs in Starbucks or Kroger, you immediately afford them more respect in your mind than if they were wearing "civilian" clothes. The same is now true in many Middle Eastern cultures. As Kumail Nanjiani jokes in the movie *The Big Sick*, the hierarchy for a good Pakistani son runs in descending order: doctor, engineer, lawyer, hundreds of jobs, ISIS, and then comedians.

Why? Medical doctors are highly valued today because of the service they provide with amazing skill—relieving pain and preventing death. Doctors have access to some magic that deals with these greatest of human fears. With learning built on a centuries-long edifice of detailed knowledge and technological abilities, medical doctors appear to work miracles, and we are all grateful for their contribution. When your child's aggressive cancer is finally beaten, knee-buckled gratitude is unavoidable. As a result, human society greatly honors medical doctors with prestige and wealth. This is all fine and good.

But there's another kind of doctor too. Indeed, before there were "medical doctors" and before MDs were the most respected people in society, another kind of doctor was regarded as the most learned and most valuable kind of person. These are the people who earned the title PhD, short for doctor of philosophy. The "doctor" part refers to the highest level of learning and the ability to teach others. The "philosophy" refers to the most important thing to learn: wisdom (*sophia*). So PhDs are lovers of wisdom, lovers of the most comprehensive understanding of the world, summed up with the word "philosophy."

We still have PhDs today, but a lot has changed. Now people can earn a PhD in countless fields of knowledge through minutely studying very specific topics: genetic pathology in sunflowers, the cultural influences on Hegel's philosophy, depressive psychology in elephants, the theme of the Latin idea of *furor* in Virgil's *Aeneid*—you name it. The PhD is a high honor, showing significant knowledge in an area. But we can understand why medical doctors seem more valuable now. Today's philosophers don't do operations. But even more disappointing, they don't even offer help with how to live daily life.

Ancient philosophers, however, did just that. Anything less than a whole-life vision for flourishing was considered a mere skill, a craft—including medicine. Olive pressing or battle-ax talent or body healing is valuable in its own limited sphere. But what we really need is wisdom for how to truly live and die well, and ancient people knew this. Philosophers alone can put all things together—knowledge of the universe, practical skills, and reflections on wisdom in relationships—into a comprehensive way of seeing and being in the world so that people could learn to thrive. This is why philosophers matter.

○ ○ ○ ○

So what happened to get us from this central role of philosophy in life and society to philosophers' minimal role in civilization today? And what in the world does this have to do with Jesus and Christianity?

To answer these questions, we must take a journey backward. We must rediscover the work and wisdom, the content and the contour of the ancient philosophers. In so doing we will learn that ancient philosophy was something very different than what it became in the modern period. And we will discover that, maybe surprisingly to us as modern readers, the Bible shares this understanding of philosophy as a way of life promising flourishing. To help us understand the Bible in this way, it is beneficial to spend a little time in Greece and Rome.

As we have already noted, philosophy in the ancient world—and our focus will be on Western civilization, rooted in the Mediterranean basin[4]—was not where smart people just played around with esoteric speculations for sport. Ancient philosophers didn't lie around at dinner parties on couches, with servants dropping grapes into their mouths, and ponder whether when a tree falls in the woods and no one hears it, it still makes a sound. Some of this did occasionally happen, I imagine, but this is not how the weighty philosophers like Socrates, Plato, Aristotle, or Seneca lived their lives.

No, philosophy in the ancient Greek and Roman world was not primarily theory and certainly not a mere focus on irrelevant speculations. Rather, it was a *way of life*, a way of being in the world. This way of being was rooted in a way of seeing or understanding how the world really is. So philosophers did ponder mysterious and big thoughts. They thought about the nature of matter and time and how the visible and invisible worlds relate. But this exploration and speculation about the nature of horses and humans and heavenly objects were always *for the purpose of helping people live a certain way*—in accord with the nature of reality—so that they might know the happiness that comes from wise living.

It would not be possible here to give a survey of the history of philosophy, or even of just the Greek philosophical tradition.

There are plenty of great books available for this purpose, and such survey is standard fare for philosophy courses in college or on YouTube. Nor would it be beneficial to survey all the disagreements between various important philosophers.

We want to ask a bigger question, not just, What happened in the history of philosophy? but rather, What *is* ancient philosophy?[5] My desire is not to present a potted history of philosophy but to get at the heart of what ancient philosophy was all about. Why was it so important to people? To make the complex world of ancient philosophy accessible and memorable, we can describe ancient philosophy's goal with two Greek words—*philosophein* (to love wisdom) and *philokalein* (to love the good).

○ ○ ○ ○

The first of our two words is where we get our word "philosophy." *Philosophein* means to love wisdom. The earliest Greek thinkers, such as Thales of Miletus, were, in modern parlance, brilliant mathematicians, biologists, astronomers, physicists, economists, urban planners, medical doctors, and statesmen. Those skilled in these areas were said to have *sophia*—wisdom.

But with Socrates and Plato and all those to follow, "philosophy" takes on a new depth. It includes these areas of study but goes beyond them *to the pursuit of a comprehensive understanding of all of the world.* Philosophy focuses on character traits and habits that, if practiced, will result in a flourishing life and society. To *sophia* (a deep knowledge of how the world works) was added the crucial idea of the art of living well.[6] It is the combination of these two—understanding and living—that becomes the focus of the great tradition of philosophy.

A couple of important ideas develop from this turn in philosophy. First, there is a recognition of the organic relationship between physics and metaphysics. "Physics" refers to the nature

of reality, how the cosmos is constructed and functions—
questions about water, fire, air, and so on—and the mathemati-
cal relationships between matter and space. Important stuff.
We still use the English word "physics" roughly this way today.

"Metaphysics," on the other hand, refers to the deepest principles of existence—being, knowing, cause, time, and space.
This is the top-level "physics" that ties all the other "physics"
together—hence, "metaphysics." Heady ideas.

The point is that, even though physics and metaphysics are
separated in the modern world, the situation in ancient philosophy was intentionally different. Physics and metaphysics were
organically related and immensely practical. Understanding
how the world is constructed and functions (physics) teaches
us who we are, what the nature of truth and time and being
are (metaphysics), and this enables us to live well. When we try
to live without knowledge of physics and metaphysics—how
the world is and works—then we are foolish, not wise, living
randomly, haphazardly, without direction or hope for security,
happiness, or peace. Sounds like a lot of people today.

In such a nonmetaphysical understanding of the world, there
is no reason to be anything other than a mere hedonist, living
for immediate pleasure. But sooner or later, thanks to pleasure's
law of diminishing returns, hedonism doesn't really satisfy or
provide a vision for individual or societal flourishing. We find
that the unexamined life isn't worth living. The tragic reality
of suicide, which is on the rise, affects the rich, famous, and
beautiful just like it does others.[7] This is despite life being better than any time in human history by nearly every measurable
metric.[8] Without a metaphysic, many find it difficult to want to
keep living, even if on the outside their lives seem good.

Today in our universities the study of physics and the exploration of big life topics such as ethics are completely separate, but they were not for the ancient philosophers. All things

are connected. The philosophers taught their hearers to study astronomy, music, and politics, because "the contemplation of harmony that reveals itself in the world of the senses . . . serves as an exercise in reaching inner harmony."[9] Moreover, the study of all aspects of knowledge became a spiritual exercise, an itinerary for spiritual growth upward that corresponded to the different parts of philosophy. Ethics clarifies the soul; physics reveals that the world has a transcendent cause; metaphysics or theology enables the contemplation of ultimate truths.[10]

○ ○ ○ ○

The second idea that comes from this ancient view of philosophy is that to learn the physics, metaphysics, and wise habits necessary for flourishing, we need *models in community*. To learn how the world works and how to live well requires teachers—people who have the capacity, training, and years of life experience, combined with virtue and integrity, who can serve as instructors *and* models. This is what a philosopher is.

Philosophers like Socrates, Plato, and Aristotle gathered disciples around them who wanted to learn their wisdom— knowledge of both what the world is and how to live practically in it. Soon this gathering of learners became formalized in schools where young men and women gathered in cities (especially Athens) to live with the philosopher and other disciples. They intentionally exercised the body and the mind, shaping habits and the heart. From the time of Plato on, it was understood that philosophy "could be carried out only by means of a community of life and dialogue between masters and disciples, within the framework of a school."[11]

It is possible to become a military pilot through a long process of enlisting and working one's way up. Far better and far more likely is doing what my brother-in-law did—go to the Air Force Academy in Colorado Springs. There, he was discipled

Figure 3. *The School of Athens* (1511) by Raphael

in all manner of things Air Force. His body, mind, habits, and vision were shaped by teachers and a very particular communal life that prepared him for his life as a fighter pilot. So too with the philosophical schools.

The ancient philosophical school is the origin of the model of education that becomes the bedrock of Western civilization. Intentional education of the whole person—body, mind, spirit—is what the Greeks called *paideia*. This is why we all had to endure gym class in junior high: education is about more than books. It is only through guided practice in all areas that one can achieve the fullness of what it means to be human, to become what they would call a *teleios anēr* (a whole/mature person). The only hope for individual and societal flourishing, the Greeks and Romans understood, was the formation of young people to see the Good by learning from teachers and models who live well. This included both knowledge and skills (the physics of the world), always situated in a metaphysic of the Good.

In such ancient philosophical schools, education happened in a community—a group of friends who loved each other and who together were building a society. The virtuous example of the philosophers/teachers who led the school was central to the entire enterprise. As Seneca would later summarize, "The living word and life in common will benefit you more than written discourse. It is to current reality that you must go, first because men believe their eyes more than their ears, and because the path of precepts is long, but that of examples is short and infallible. . . . It was not Epicurus' school which made great men of Metrodorus, Hermarchus, and Polyaenus, but his companionship."[12]

○ ○ ○ ○

Long before *Wicked* became a Broadway hit, Stephen Schwartz had already made his musical career and fortune with *Godspell*, followed by film scores for *Pocahontas*, *The Hunchback of Notre Dame*, and *The Prince of Egypt*. But the popularity of *Wicked* is so great now that it will likely be the musical Schwartz is most remembered for. And rightly so. *Wicked* has been running on Broadway continually since 2003 and is regularly staged in sold-out theaters all over the world.

What is *Wicked* about? In short, it is a prequel to the famous story *The Wizard of Oz*. But it is also subversive. It is a retelling of the origin story of the Wicked Witch of the West, revealing that things are not always as they seem. The "witch" was once a girl with a name, Elphaba, who experienced various traumas that shaped her. And it turns out that she was wrongly labeled "wicked" by unscrupulous leaders.

Wicked is truly a genius piece of musical storytelling. But at the very core of the whole musical is one driving idea—*What are goodness and happiness?* You won't necessarily pick this up at the first viewing or even on the fiftieth listening to the delightful soundtrack. But with powerful subtlety, Schwartz has woven the philosophical question of goodness and happiness throughout the story from beginning to end.

The title *Wicked* is the first clue, especially once you realize that the whole story is seeking to challenge our blind following of leaders who spin goodness and evil in deceptive ways. The first word of the whole story is "good," sung in a song espousing the "good news" that the wicked witch is now dead. The question of true goodness continues throughout and appears explicitly in the dialogue, and especially in the songs "Thank Goodness," "No Good Deed," and the poignant final duet, "For Good." A search through the lyrics for "happiness" shows this as the other side of the same philosophical coin that is deposited in the musical.

Schwartz is a profoundly thoughtful and creative person, and he is inviting people to see the beauty and happiness in finding the Good. He also challenges us to not be hoodwinked into thinking we can access such goodness in popularity, superficial romance, or merely trying to "dance through life" without facing reality. Schwartz's *Wicked* is a powerful piece of musical philosophy.

○ ○ ○ ○

Thinking about ancient Greek education and Schwartz's modern-day musical on the Good leads us to the second of our verbal hooks on which we will hang our understanding of ancient philosophy—*philokalein*, to love the good and beautiful. In the earliest, most famous (and in many people's opinion still the best) book on ethics, Aristotle starts with this sentence: "Every art and every inquiry, and similarly every action and pursuit, is thought to aim at some good; and for this reason the Good has rightly been declared to be that at which all things aim."[13]

Aristotle goes into a lengthy and nuanced exploration of what the Good is, how to pursue it, and how to live accordingly, all so that his son might find a truly happy life. This is ethics: discerning, pursuing, and experiencing the fruits of what is good and beautiful. This is more than theoretical exploration; it's also intensely practical. It is right at the heart of the whole philosophical enterprise.

This approach to ethics focuses on developing the character of the person to know and love the Good. This is called virtue (from *virtus*, human/man), because it is only through the development of one's habits and character in accordance with the Good that one can enter into the fullness of human potential and flourishing, to become fully human. Education is being released from the cave of darkness into the true light of the knowledge of the Good so that one can live fully and teach others to do the same.[14] Many centuries later, Dante Alighieri summed up this vision with the famous words, "Consider your origin: You were not formed to live like brutes, but to follow virtue and knowledge."[15]

Under this umbrella idea of the Good and with the Good as the foundation and the goal, ancient philosophy explored many topics. The map of *philokalein* (loving the Good) was investigated on four main compass points:

- Metaphysics—What is the true nature of the universe, and how does the world work?
- Epistemology—How do we know things?
- Ethics—What is right, and how do we live it out?
- Politics—How do we structure society and institutions in the best and wisest ways?

These four compass points provide a map for the land of the Good, with the goal of creating human flourishing or "the

Good Life." Philosophers questioned and explored each of these realms in increasing detail, with the result being ever-longer books. Then later writers wrote books about these books. This is all good, and we still study what Socrates had to say about knowing and what Aristotle had to say about ethics and what Plato had to say about the nature of ideas and how to structure society. But the focus on the details of *what* these philosophers said has tended to obscure what they actually cared the most about—*why* they explored these issues. Their philosophies were for the purpose of knowing and living in accord with the Good.

Ancient philosophy can be described then, surprisingly to us, as "spiritual exercises," practices in life that are informed by reflections, with the focus on learned practical wisdom for the inner person.[16] We might even describe ancient philosophy as therapy for the soul, providing practical guidance for both the individual and society. All of this is possible because of the commitment to pursue the Good. This is what we mean when we talk about "the Good Life" (like in the subtitle of this book). The Good Life is not referring to the lives of the rich and famous as revealed in a tabloid or exposé show. The Good Life refers to the habits of practiced wisdom that produce in the human soul deep and lasting flourishing.

○ ○ ○ ○

This all sounds wonderful and helpful. And this is why Greek and then Roman society was in many ways so advanced. This is why we are still reading the books written by the ancient thinkers, while most of the books written today will be forgotten within a few years at best. This is why the founders of modern nations, including the United States, got their inspiration and ideas from ancient philosophers. Thomas Jefferson had a copy of Seneca on his nightstand when he died. This kind of philosophy matters.

So what in the world happened such that philosophers went from being the sculptors of society to being the esoteric teachers in dwindling university departments? Why does every parent dread hearing at Christmas break that their college son or daughter has decided to major in philosophy? What happened to philosophy?

We began the chapter with Steve Martin's quip about philosophy screwing us up for the rest of our lives. Some philosophers today have recognized the problem with modern philosophy. Arguably the most influential modern philosopher, Immanuel Kant, highlights the problem with his field: "The ancient Greek philosophers, such as Epicurus, Zeno, and Socrates, remained more faithful to the Idea of the philosopher than their modern counterparts have done. 'When will you finally begin to *live* virtuously?' said Plato to an old man who told him he was attending classes on virtue. The point is not always to speculate, but also ultimately to think about applying our knowledge. Today, however, he who lives in conformity with what he teaches is taken for a dreamer."[17]

Or more succinctly, Henry David Thoreau opines that "there are nowadays professors of philosophy, but not philosophers." That is, philosophers today tell us about philosophy but have little desire to teach a comprehensive vision of happiness nor serve as models themselves. The stories of ethics professors coming to a miserable end by hooking up with graduate students thirty years their junior are a sadly common reality. Thoreau continues with his emphasis that a real philosopher *lives* as a philosopher: "To be a philosopher is not merely to have subtle thoughts, nor even to found a school, but so to love wisdom as to live according to its dictates, a life of simplicity, independence, magnanimity."[18]

So what happened? Why is our experience and understanding of philosophy so different today than it was in the ancient world? The full answer to this would be as long and thick and complicated as the story of the history of Western thought, politics, education, and religion over the last two thousand years—a Herculean task that goes far beyond our goal here. But we can briefly trace the journey from a satellite view.

In one sense, ancient philosophy never went away. But it continued in a place that unfortunately got separated from the rest of culture, including the rest of Christianity—the monasteries. The ancient philosophical schools of people living together and dedicated to a life of virtuous learning is where the patristic and medieval monastic traditions come from.

In broader society, cracks in the ancient philosophical approach began to appear especially during the Enlightenment of the 1700s. The rise of the modern "scientific" university that followed sealed the deal for separating philosophers from a life of practiced virtue.

○ ○ ○ ○

Today, key aspects of ancient philosophical reflection on the whole world are peeled away and shipped off to other intellectual departments—cosmology goes to physics, ethics to religion or as a blip in a practical field ("business ethics" in an MBA), language to linguistics, and human habits become the purview of neuroscience and psychology. Modern philosophy comprises mostly professors talking about the history of philosophy.

There are a few original philosophers who wrestle with big ideas such as epistemology and language, but typically this is done without a clear and comprehensive metaphysic. The idea that such philosophical reflections are connected to a committed way of life ("spiritual exercises") is nonsensical in the modern world. While a doctor of philosophy degree in any field still garners some unquantifiable respect, these "doctors" (complete with scare quotes) aren't the kind "that really help anybody," compared to the medical doctor. Those of us with children and a PhD have had to painfully explain to our kids at some point that we're not "real" doctors.

Today's philosophers have little interest in weighing into such politically charged issues that make universal claims about society. Those who do, like Roger Scruton, get shot at with multiple guns. And even if a thinker today provides some insight into an aspect of life—such as finances, relationships, or physical health—this is a limited sphere. Philosophers today rarely operate with a metaphysic comprehensive enough to offer a whole vision for life. That's only for "religious" people, whose role in society is intentionally circumscribed.

Well, almost no philosophers attempt to do so. Today there are a very few exceptions—exceptions that prove the rule. We can think of one or two public thinkers who are offering something closer to a whole-life philosophy than we encounter in society today. As of this writing, we are a few years in to what I call the JPP—the Jordan Peterson Phenomenon. Jordan Peterson, a professor of psychology at the University of Toronto, has written an international bestseller entitled *12 Rules for Life: An Antidote to Chaos*, and he has well over two million subscribers to his YouTube channel that is loaded with videos of him exploring psychology, feminism, economic systems, societal structure, virtue and goodness, religion and the Bible, and so on.

As one measure of Peterson's widespread influence in society, in April 2019 he had a formal debate with another public thinker, Slavoj Žižek. Not only did people go, but tickets were sold as if to a sporting event or rock concert. Tickets were so in demand that on the day of the event they were being scalped at prices higher than the National Hockey League playoff game between the Maple Leafs and Bruins that same night! Peterson is controversial, to say the least, and often derided for overstepping his expertise and for strongly challenging many aspects of the modern status quo. Some of these critiques are fair, some are not.

But Peterson's popularity and comprehensiveness—he suggests twelve rules for living the Good Life—is the remarkable exception in today's philosophical world. Peterson is precisely what every philosopher longs for in terms of impact (or at least the financial benefits of his book sales). He is so well known largely because no one else has had the audacity to offer such a comprehensive vision for living well. In the ancient world this is what all philosophers did. The fact that we know Peterson so well is partly because of how rare it is to meet someone today who is offering a comprehensive philosophy. The television philosopher Oprah might be the most comparable persona, though without the educational clout of Peterson.

Why does this matter? It matters because this shift away from philosophers having a sculpting effect on people with a focus on the Good is a loss—a loss to individuals and thereby to culture itself. Yet we continue to try to live and build societies without a clear metaphysic, without a clear structure of virtue and character formation.

○ ○ ○ ○

One of the most interesting and comedically profound television shows in recent years is *The Good Place*, starring Ted Danson and Kristen Bell. The basic premise of the show is that the main characters all die and arrive in this wonderful town, "The Good Place," because they are being rewarded according to how well they lived and how much good they did, based on a points system. These characters all have enough points to enter this wonderful afterlife.

The deep theme going on throughout the whole show, reflected in the title, is the question of what it means to be good. According to the writers, originally the show was planned to be an exploration of how different religions defined what was good. The religious question only comes up in the first episode. When Eleanor

Shellstrop (Kristen Bell's character) arrives in this utopian town, she meets the guy in charge, Michael, and she just *has* to ask which religion on earth was right. In a very funny scene, Michael points to a cheesy-looking painting behind his desk of a normal-looking dude and tells Eleanor, "Hindus are a little bit right, Muslims a little bit. Jews, Christians, Buddhists, every religion guessed about 5 percent, except for Doug Forcett. Doug was a stoner kid who lived in Calgary during the 1970s. One night, he got really high on mushrooms, and his best friend, Randy, said, 'Hey, what do you think happens after we die?' And Doug just launched into this long monologue where he got like 92 percent correct."[19]

As the writers developed the show, they decided instead to approach the question of the Good from a philosophical perspective rather than a religious one. And so, instead of using religions, in each episode they have a hearty discussion of real philosophers and philosophies. One of the characters was in life a philosophy professor—who turns out to struggle greatly to live his own beliefs—and he gives lectures on how different philosophies wrestle with what it means to be and do good. Sounds boring, I realize, but it's so well done, so funny, and with such beloved characters that it works.

The Good Place seamlessly weds philosophical (ethics, epistemology, metaphysics) and religious ideas (the afterlife and what it means to be righteous) because these two worlds never used to be separate, nor should they be. Religion in the ancient world was not primarily a set of beliefs to be cognitively acknowledged but an allegiance to a certain God or gods that showed you how to see the world and how to be in the world so that you might find life and flourishing. So too was ancient philosophy. Philosophy was an allegiance to a certain way of seeing and being in the world, learned and lived in community for the purpose of finding the Good Life.

THE BIBLE AS
PHILOSOPHY?

The Philosophical "Big Ideas" in the Old Testament

Remember that church in Dura-Europos with its pictures of Jesus as a philosopher? Not far down the street in the same ancient town there was a synagogue, a gathering place for metropolitan third-century Jews. Throughout this beautifully decorated space, various scenes from Israel's history encircled the faithful.[1] Most of these pictures feature the greatest man in Israel's history, Moses. No fewer than seven scenes from Moses's life appear in the Dura-Europos synagogue. And how is he depicted? The answer may be surprising: Moses is dressed in a toga, with the posture, haircut, and beard that show him clearly to be a great philosopher. The Christians weren't alone.

Moses a philosopher? Wasn't he a prophet? A miracle worker? The famous lawgiver of the Ten Commandments? Yes, he was all those things, but for the worshipers in the Dura-Europos synagogue, this didn't exclude him from being a philosopher (see fig. 4). In fact, if we could ask the faithful Jewish wall painter who depicted Moses this way, he would be ready with an answer. It is precisely *because* of Moses's teaching and ruling roles that he should be considered a philosopher. Moses was the one whom God used in a special way to rescue God's people

Public Domain / Wikimedia Commons

Figure 4. Wall painting of Moses and the burning bush from Dura-Europos

and then give them instructions on how to live life together so that they might know God's favor. This is what it means to be a philosopher of God.

The synagogue painters in Dura-Europos were not alone. Already by the first century BC, Jewish people were talking about the sixteenth-century-BC Moses in this way—Moses was a great philosopher long before Socrates and company even came on the scene. The ancient author Philo of Alexandria (ca. 20 BC–AD 50) was a Jew trained as a Greek philosopher, and he readily interpreted Moses this way. The "of Alexandria" in his name shows that Philo was shaped by one of the greatest educational systems of the ancient world, that of the city of Alexandria, Egypt. The "Philo" part of his name is not Jewish but Greek, a pointer to the fact that he loved wisdom (*philosophia*) and also that he loved God. Philo left us with many writings showing his deep piety and dedication to God's revelation in the Bible. For him it was natural to speak of Moses as a philosopher.

Philo understood the Jewish synagogues in terms of Greek *paideia* (whole-person education), because they are doing the same thing—they are schools of virtue that train people to see the world and be in the world in certain ways. The rabbinic schools of Jesus's day were modeled on the Greek philosophical schools. One of Philo's most important arguments along these lines is that Moses was in fact a great philosopher. Moses spoke of the great mysteries of the world, he gave laws from God to enable people to live well, and he ruled over God's people with great wisdom. He was, in short, the ancient ideal of what a leader should be—not a mere politician but a philosopher-king, sage, prophet, and priest from God. Early Christians picked up on these same arguments and used them to argue for the ancient wisdom of the Jewish-Christian tradition.

We saw in the previous chapter that ancient philosophers taught a way of seeing and being in the world that promised human flourishing through learning what the Good is. Was Philo right that Moses was a philosopher? Yes! And Moses is not alone in the Old Testament. Moses and his writings are the foundation of the rest of the Bible for a great truth that we have forgotten in modern times—*that the Hebrew Scriptures present themselves as a work of divinely revealed ancient philosophy.*

The orthodox Israeli scholar Yoram Hazony has been one of the strongest voices arguing for a rediscovery of this idea—the philosophical reading of the Hebrew Scriptures.[2] Hazony observes that the modern turn in the study of philosophy has created a false distinction between reason and revelation, between philosophy and faith. This prejudice against revelation and faith has blinded modern people from recognizing that the Hebrew Scriptures do actually present themselves as a philosophy of life in the ancient sense. As Hazony points out, the Bible's claims to be rooted in the revelation of God do not disqualify it from providing a philosophy worth examining. The idea that a book can't be considered philosophy because it claims to be revealed is "nothing but a bare prejudice."[3]

Hazony seeks to show that the Hebrew Scriptures can and should be read as works of philosophy, with readers seeking to hear what the Scriptures have to say about the nature of the world and how humans should live justly.[4] In other words, the Hebrew Bible can be read fruitfully as an ancient (and still-relevant) philosophical work.

In our previous discussion of ancient philosophy, we identified four compass points by which ancient people explored the Good and how to pursue the Good Life—metaphysics, epistemology, ethics, and politics. When we read the Old Testament we see that these four issues are discussed extensively.

○ ○ ○ ○

Metaphysics. Metaphysics in philosophy deals with what are often called first principles—the big abstract ideas of being, nature, time, identity, and cause. Or more simply, What is the true nature of the universe, and how does the world work? Does the Old Testament address these issues? Very much so. To hear the metaphysical music of the Bible, let's start at the very beginning, a very good place to start. The very beginning of the Bible's story is an account of how everything came to be, the creation account of Genesis, a metaphysic extraordinaire.

Ancient people had various views on how the world was created, typically through the combination, conflict, or consummation of ancient gods or forces, such as the Egyptian Geb and Nut, whose sexual union formed and frames the world. There were a lot of gods hanging around in ancient Near Eastern minds—gods of rain, fertility, war, agriculture. Subsequently, most ancient people were polytheists, believing in various gods that ruled different aspects of human life and the world.

But not the Hebrew people. What sets the ancient faith of the Hebrews apart is their radical claim that there is only *one* true God, who spoke and created the whole universe by his own power, and that this same God is active in controlling and sustaining all of his creation. All other "gods"—and there are other spiritual beings—are actually created beings who are subservient to the God of the Hebrews. And very importantly, this one God is benevolent and personal, revealing himself and caring for his creatures and creation.

This is what we see in the first pages of the Bible, in the account of the genesis of the world. We meet a singular personal deity who has a counsel of created beings around him and who speaks the world into being by the power of his mouth. His Spirit is hovering over the primordial chaos of the watery world and then, "*Yehi or!*"—Let there be light! And there was. God continues to create and form the world over the course of six days, and then he rests, declaring it all to be Good (not an accident that this is the same word we saw in ancient philosophy).

This description of the nature of reality is a bold and important claim that sets the key and rhythm for the music of the whole Bible. The biblical metaphysic is that the world does not consist of mysterious and impersonal forces that are in conflict with each other and striving for dominance or balance (such as a yin-yang dualism). The world is not an impersonal mixture of various atomic elements such as fire and water. Rather, the world is one consistent reality, because it comes from one personal and kind God who exercises sovereign and wise control over the whole world. This metaphysic of creation also means that there are key distinctions in place—distinctions between the Creator and his creatures, between the Creator and creation, and between human creatures (who alone are made in God's own image) and other created beings (such as animals), unlike many belief systems that blend these.

The creation story is foundational, but it's not the whole story. Very soon—only three chapters in—Genesis tells us that the creation has undergone a breaking, a disruption. This means that our experience of the world is not as it was originally designed nor where it will finally end up. The fall and the promised restoration of creation are central to the Hebrew metaphysic of nature, because the world is not trapped in a cyclical state. The narrative of the Bible is a linear story with a beginning, middle, and end yet to come. In other words, the Hebrew Scriptures have great interest in providing a clear metaphysical description of the world and where it is going.

If God created only an inanimate world or a world with conscienceless creatures, then we wouldn't need a metaphysical discussion. But we exist and we think and we wonder and we struggle and we suffer. The same creation account in Genesis describes not only how the physical world came into being but also how humans were made. Humans are not a random assortment of atoms, the result of various elemental forces, or the offspring of the mating of certain gods. Rather, humans were made male and female in the image of the one true God, after the pattern of God's own uncreated being. The Hebrew metaphysic concerning humanity means that as bearers of God's image and commissioned with a role of tending God's creation, humans have inherent worth and meaning. Even with the corrupting effects of the fall, this value and purpose for humanity remains—the image of God is marred but not obliterated. This is a very sophisticated metaphysic of the world.

○ ○ ○ ○

Epistemology. To be human is to be conscious and to think. A sign of maturing humanity is when a person begins to be aware of their own thinking processes. Since ancient times, humans have been engaged in such meta-thinking—thinking about thinking. The Greek tradition particularly highlights this awareness of meta-thinking, with Socrates famously emphasizing that he actually knows nothing—the way to wisdom is to become aware of one's own lack of knowledge. Epistemology concerns reflections on how we know things and how to evaluate what is right and wrong and what is true and false.

Once again, we see that the Hebrew Scriptures show keen awareness of this kind of philosophical question and speak directly to it. What knowledge is and how we obtain it is a major theme throughout the Bible. Unlike our modern conception of "knowing," which conceives knowledge as the objective possession of facts, in both the Hebrew and Greek worlds knowing is intimately related to experiencing, even to having a personal relationship. "Knowledge" in the Bible is practical and living, obtained by experience and resulting in a change of who we are. "Know" can even be used to describe the most intimate of interpersonal relations possible—sexual intimacy (Gen. 4:1; Matt. 1:25). Indeed, it is probably best to speak of the verb "knowing" more than the noun "knowledge," because knowing is a *process* of learning to see in a certain way. To know is to experience.[5]

Issues of epistemology in the Hebrew Scriptures start with the biblical creation account, where the tree forbidden to Adam and Eve concerns the "knowledge of good and evil." This tree represents a kind of knowledge that was the possession of God alone. By partaking of the fruit of this tree in disobedience to God's command, the first humans simultaneously grew in awareness while also becoming darkened in their understanding and wills because of the broken relationship with their Creator.

The subsequent story of Israel, which takes up most of the space of the Old Testament, can be described as a cyclical story of *knowing God, forgetting God,* and *coming to know God again.* Time and again God's people went through seasons and generations of intimacy and true worship of God through listening to his instructions and obeying his revelation. These are followed by times of neglect or rejection of the knowledge of God. The result of this was foolishness, suffering, and judgment.

God continually sent prophets to call his people back to a true knowledge of him that came through obedience to what he commanded. The prophets proclaim that God's people are *not* flourishing and are on a path of destruction precisely because they do not *know* God rightly and intimately. This is stated over and over by prophets such as Isaiah (1:3; 5:13; 44:18–19; 45:4–5, 20; 47:10; 56:10; 59:8) and Jeremiah (2:8, 19; 4:22; 5:4; 8:7; 9:6; 14:18), as well as several times in the minor prophets (e.g., Mic. 4:12).[6] In one striking example, the foreign king Nebuchadnezzar is divinely judged for his arrogance and is turned into a hairy, long-clawed beast in the wilderness until he comes to *know* and *acknowledge* that the God of Israel rules over all (Dan. 4:25, 32; 5:21). Then he is restored to his humanity. What a powerful picture of proper knowledge and its relationship to virtue (being human) not vice (being vicious, animallike).

The book of Hosea also stands out as a good example of this theme.[7] Hosea lived and prophesied in a very tumultuous time, and he understood Israel's catastrophic situation to be divine chastisement for her sins. Hosea provides a piercing diagnosis of what Israel's spiritual malady is—it is a lack of *knowledge* of God: "My people are destroyed for lack of knowledge. Because you have rejected knowledge, I also reject you as my priests; because you have ignored the law of your God, I also will ignore your children" (4:6; see also 4:1; 5:4; 11:3).[8]

The solution to this spiritual brokenness corresponds logically. Israel's need is to *know the Lord*, as we find in several passages (Hosea 2:20; 14:9), including the beautiful summary prayer-exhortation: "Let us acknowledge the LORD; let us press on to acknowledge him. As surely as the sun rises, he will appear; he will come to us like winter rains, like the spring rains that water the earth" (6:3). We should press on to know the Lord because, though shocking to hear in light of the sacrificial system that God has ordained, God cares more about mercy and faithfulness than he does about sacrifice, about the knowledge of God more than burnt offerings (6:6).

So the Hebrew Scriptures, like the rest of ancient philosophy, very clearly focus on the central role that self-aware knowing plays in what it means to live well. One portion of the Old Testament—the Wisdom literature (Proverbs, Job, Ecclesiastes)—particularly focuses on the related epistemological question of *how* one comes to know. In many ways the book of Proverbs is the quintessential place to turn to when asking about the Bible and knowledge. This is because the whole point of Proverbs is to provide succinct and pithy knowledge about how to live wisely and virtuously in the world. And from the very beginning of the book, it is stated clearly that this way of wisdom and knowledge is possible only if one is oriented rightly toward God—"The fear of the LORD is the beginning of knowledge, but fools despise wisdom and instruction" (Prov. 1:7).[9]

This sets the parameters for what true knowledge and wisdom is for all of Scripture. True knowledge is not merely a matter of assembling and compiling facts, having knowledge in a "scientific" sense. Rather, knowledge (which leads to wisdom) is a function of a relationship with God. As one scholar has wisely noted, "The fear of the Lord is the key to Israel's epistemology [knowing] . . . , for knowing the Creator puts one in position appropriately to know the creation and humans with their divinely given possibilities and limits."[10]

The questions of knowing in the Old Testament are very sophisticated and nuanced. We mentioned how Proverbs gives principles for wise living that are rooted in the fear of the Lord. At the same time, the Hebrew Scriptures acknowledge that life is complicated and confusing. Proverbs provides paradigms of general wisdom for life, but the story of Job sensitively shows that life is more complicated than pithy wisdom sayings—there is suffering that is often inexplicable and unjust. Thus wisdom includes a recognition of the limits of our understanding and our need to trust God even in the midst of the pain and confusion of suffering. The book of Ecclesiastes likewise overflows the banks of the simple understanding of the book of Proverbs. The author of Ecclesiastes faces the great existential question that any person who has lived a while will eventually face: Is life really predictable and meaningful, or is everything random and fleeting emptiness? Comparable to Job, the book faces these complex questions head-on and finally concludes that living according to God-fearing wisdom is the only way forward.[11] Once again we see the Hebrew Scriptures are engaging in philosophy.

○ ○ ○ ○

Ethics. The question of what the Good is drives all of ancient philosophy. The subcategory of ethics addresses specifically how to live in accord with the Good such that one can live well. This central focus in philosophy once again finds a parallel in the Hebrew Scriptures.

The God of the Bible works out his interaction with humanity through a series of covenants—God-initiated reciprocal relationships. God has all the power and glory, and he gives benefaction to his beloved creatures. The reciprocal response of humans to this benefactor covenant is called torah. "Torah" in English has come to be translated as "law," but this is a bit off. "Covenantal instructions" would be better. The German language has a great word that could be used here too, *Lebensordnung*—structure or way of life. God's torah consists of specific instructions for lots of situations—for example, when someone crashes his ox cart into your house. Torah contains ethical teachings and instructions about what is right and wrong (think the Ten Commandments), how to properly relate to God (think Leviticus), and how to properly handle relationships in the community, especially when something has gone wrong (think Numbers and Deuteronomy). But a covenantal relationship with God is just that—a *relationship*—and so the ethics of the Bible are from beginning to end characterized by relating to God and each other in ways that accord with God's own nature.

In this way the ethics of the Hebrew Scriptures very much accord with ancient Greek and Roman philosophy—not always on the specifics of what the Good *is*, but on the focus on ethics as being about virtue. This means that the ethical teaching of the ancient world was not *voluntaristic* (the right thing to do is whatever is commanded) nor *deontological* (the right is based on principles that have nothing to do with the person) but *virtuous*, meaning that the *character of the person* must be formed according to the Good. An ethics of virtue, which is shared by ancient philosophy and the Bible, focuses on the development of our sensibilities, values, and habits. Virtue teaches people to live *wisely* so that, in the great variety of life experiences, we will be able to discern what the Good is in each circumstance.

What distinguishes the Hebrew Scripture's virtue ethic from others in the ancient world is its focus on this ethic coming through the revelation of a personal, covenantal God. But the Hebrew Scriptures share the same focus on virtue.

○ ○ ○ ○

Politics. The word "politics" has become loaded with negative connotations in modern English, evoking images of backroom deals, posturing, power grabbing, and polarizing rhetoric. There have always been bad politicians and bad governments, but this does not have to necessarily be so. "Politics" doesn't have to be a negative word. Our word "politics" has its origins in something much more positive and constructive: the Greek philosophical reflection on how the Good should be worked out in society, in relationships between individuals, and in how to build a society that will inculcate flourishing and the Good Life for its citizens (Greek, *politeia*).

This idea of *politeia* has been the basis for democratic- and republic-based governments in Western civilization for millennia. This older, constructive sense of "politics" was a natural and crucial aspect of the ancient philosophical perspective because the philosophers understood that (1) flourishing is not possible apart from societal stability and structures that promoted beauty, goodness, and virtue; and (2) humans need each other to flourish.

Indeed, it was not good for the first human to be alone, as we learn in the second chapter of Genesis, even before the fall (Gen. 2:18). Human flourishing can be found fully only in relationships. Humans need friends. Consequently, the Hebrew Scriptures are very keen on providing a political philosophy or vision for how to structure society for the Good. This vision, like the Old Testament's metaphysic, epistemology, and ethics, is rooted in the revelation of the personal God to his creation.

Most of the torah concerns relationships between humans. Of course, portions of God's instructions focus on the vertical relationship of humanity toward God. But the torah puts great emphasis also on the horizontal—on interpersonal relationships and the relationships of individuals to societal structures. We can see this in shorthand form in the Ten Commandments, which are divided into two tablets. Commands 1–4 concern relationship with God, while commands 5–10 are about relating to each other (Exod. 20:1–17). Hebrew tradition has summarized all of torah with two comprehensive required loves—love for God and love for neighbor (Deut. 6:4–5; Lev. 19:17–18). Forming a loving *politeia* is essential to life.

The height of Israel's political state occurred under King David. The instructions God gave for kingdom conduct were rooted in God's own nature. Of course, people groups and empires that were contemporary with Israel also had a vision for how to structure society. But the Hebrew political philosophy is strikingly beautiful in comparison. As Yoram Hazony points out, the unification of the twelve tribes of Israel into one political entity under a king who remains humble and treats his kinsmen as a brother is very different from the surrounding ancient Near Eastern imperial states. In other ancient kingdoms there were no divine-ethical limits on territorial ambitions, or the size of the military, or the amount of resources that the king could extract from the subjects in taxes and forced labor. The emperors were often worshiped as gods.[12]

But the God of Israel put limits on all his appointed human kings. Ultimately, God was the real king of Israel, and any appointed kings were his sons, not independent sovereigns. Of course, to have an organized government, some degree of power and sovereignty must be invested in the human king. But the Hebrew vision for the political state set limits on all of this. The Hebrews' ultimate allegiance was to God himself, not to the human king. The human king and other leaders were brothers and coworshipers of the one true God. This is a *politeia* rooted in the just and good way.

This divinely revealed political philosophy was not just for the sake of the Hebrew people but was also a model for all the nations. It is a picture of how the true God has structured the cosmos and the means by which humans may experience flourishing or shalom. It is easy to miss this because of the Hebrew-centricity of the Mosaic covenant. But, as the Hebrew Scriptures make clear, the God of Israel is not just the benefactor of the Hebrews; he is also the kind Creator of the whole world. Therefore, if the God of Israel "is indeed the god and benefactor of all the earth, then his actions, commands, and pronouncements, unlike those of the other tribal or national gods known to the ancient world, must in some way be a reflection of that which is good, not only for this or that nation, but for all mankind."[13]

This investigation into the nature of the Good in the moral and political realms is precisely what the Greek and Roman philosophers were keen to explore and was a crucial part of *philosophia*. Major works such as Plato's *Republic* and Aristotle's *Politics* dealt with precisely the same issues, and these works were central to ancient philosophy's contribution to society. In the Old Testament, God is revealing to his creation through the Hebrews what the Good is and what offers true life (Deut. 29:28; 30:11–15). This is a revelation of what justice and righteousness is. Israel stands as a model for the world of "a certain way of life, . . . a certain way of looking at the world," a philosophy.[14]

○ ○ ○ ○

Earlier, we met Yoram Hazony, the Israeli scholar who argues convincingly for a philosophical reading of the Hebrew Scriptures. With the keen insight of an orthodox Jew steeped in the study of the Scriptures, Hazony provides a fascinating account of how the canon of the Hebrew Bible is intentionally structured. The books that constitute the "history of Israel" (Genesis through Kings, with Deuteronomy as central) are the base for the whole vision of the rest of the Bible. On this base, the goal of the Hebrew Scriptures, Hazony argues, is to show that "Israel stands for a certain way of life, and a certain way of looking at the world."[15] This particular way of life and way of looking at the world has a goal: that through learning God's ways, the whole world might be blessed. In other words, God has given his wisdom to Israel, which must maintain its faithfulness to this true vision of the world, so that they can be the conduit of this blessed way to all nations. The point of the whole Bible is to give wisdom that leads to life in his kingdom.

Thus, the Hebrew Scriptures provide "a general account of the nature of the moral and political order," "the provision of a general account of why 'life and the good' have escaped the nations, and of how mankind may attain them nonetheless." *The point of the history of Israel is not simply to give facts about historical events but to cast a vision of the true and the good for all the world.* This goal of exploring and explaining what constitutes the Good Life for individuals and society is, as we have seen, precisely what the Greeks called *philosophia*. The Hebrew Scriptures / Old Testament are providing a philosophy for the world.[16]

○ ○ ○ ○

And now we are arriving at our destination. The Hebrew Scriptures are given to provide the true, divinely revealed answers to these great human questions. To quote Hazony once more, the Hebrew Scriptures exist "to establish political, moral, and metaphysical truths of a general nature" and apply these to the Jewish people and then beyond.[17]

The point of all of this reflection is that these big philosophical ideas in ancient philosophy are not found only there. Rather, the same ideas prove to be very important to the story and theology of the Old Testament. The Hebrew Scriptures provide a divinely revealed metaphysic, epistemology, virtue ethic, and political philosophy based on the ultimate Good, God himself. This revelation is for the good of humanity, to shape and train humanity to see and be in the world in the particular ways that alone promise true flourishing and happiness because they are rooted in God's nature. "Happy is the person who does not walk in the counsel of the wicked . . . , but whose delight is in the Torah of God and who meditates on it day and night. This person will be like a tree planted by streams of water that yields its fruit in season and whose leaf does not wither—whatever they do flourishes!" (Ps. 1:1–3, my translation). Moses was a philosopher. The prophets were (often fiery) philosophers. The psalmists were philosophers. Solomon was a philosopher. They all offer wisdom for life.

○○○○

Dallas Willard was one of the twentieth century's great minds and great hearts. He lived a long and productive life, full of joys and sorrows. From a humble boyhood in the Missouri dustbowl to his renown as a philosopher at the University of Southern California, Willard was a faithful minister with a sharp and winsome intellect. As a graduate student at Baylor University in the late 1950s, Willard came to see something that forever marked his life and ministry—that the vocations of preaching, teaching, and philosophy were not and need not be separated. Willard saw that the Bible was addressing the big philosophical questions of life. He articulated it this way: "You look at the fundamental teachings of the Old Testament; for example, [the commandant of] having no other [gods] before you. This attempts to address the same questions as philosophy. The two main issues in philosophy have been historically, who is well off and who is a really good person, and those run together and they push you to the question, what is real. That is what the Bible is about. The need to see what the questions are is what is commonly over-looked."[18]

Who is "well off," "who is a really good person," and "what is real" are Willard's humble and accessible ways of describing to laypeople what he knew to be the great philosophical questions: What is happiness/flourishing? What is goodness? and What is reality? As Willard's biographer goes on to paraphrase, "The Bible presents us with answers to these fundamental, philosophical questions. In the Bible, God is the ultimate reality, and one is a good person and truly well off when one is in a right relationship to God." The Bible is addressing precisely the same questions as traditional philosophy.[19]

The Philosophical "Big Ideas" in the New Testament

What did Jesus look like? People have been using art to answer that question for two thousand years. All of us have some mental image of Jesus's appearance, probably shaped by a picture we saw as a child or a painting that is familiar in our culture, like Warner Sallman's *Christ at Heart's Door* (see fig. 5 for one nineteenth-century example). In modern America this image presents to us a relatively attractive Jesus with nicely defined facial features; long, well-combed brown hair with a bit of a sheen; and full-length robes. In your mind's eye he probably has a benign expression that is serene and kind, though probably not laughing. But what did Jesus actually look like?

We can't know for sure, but we can be reasonably certain he looked not so much like a modern painting but like an olive-skinned, underfed first-century Mediterranean Jew—because this is what he was. Recently, scientists have used DNA and bone samples to digitally re-create something close to what an average man of Jesus's time and place would have looked like.[1] The results are not quite what our modern images have been—he wouldn't be on the cover of *GQ* or even the front of the VBS curriculum.

Figure 5. Traditional depiction of Jesus from the late nineteenth century (artist unknown)

So even though we can't know for sure what Jesus looked like, we can ask another important question: How did people *present* Jesus's appearance in the first several centuries of

Christianity? Throughout the Middle Ages in Europe, he was often portrayed as very somber—a dour, long-faced Jesus either serenely teaching, or performing a miracle, or writhing in pain on a cross. Alternately, Jesus was often depicted as the risen and ruling king, fully robed and with the crown of thorns replaced with a golden diadem and scepter.

But what about in the earliest centuries of the Christian faith? How was Jesus depicted in early Christian art? This matters because how Jesus was painted or mosaicked or sculpted reveals much about how he was understood by his earliest followers and worshipers.

In her book *What Did Jesus Look Like?*, Joan Taylor explores this question. The short answer is that in the earliest centuries Jesus was depicted in one of two ways—as a philosopher or as a king. In the first instance, it is easy to see that Jesus was depicted as a philosopher because of how frequently philosophers were portrayed in paintings, mosaics, and sculpture. Remember Dura-Europos. In the Roman Empire in the first couple of centuries AD, philosophers were presented in fairly standard ways, typically wearing a wrapped garment that covered the left shoulder with the right shoulder bare. Philosophers were posed as looking ahead, not triumphantly but with confidence, or as holding a scroll and thoughtfully looking at it. Sometimes philosophers would be seated, since teachers taught from this position, but never on a cushioned, jewel-encrusted throne like an emperor. The hairstyles varied by century and fashion, sometimes long and shaggy, sometimes short and clipped, and beards came and went as fashions changed. But it was always clear who the sculpted philosophers were and the role they played as sculptors of society.[2] In the context of these widespread iconic images of philosophers, we find standardized images of Jesus, short-haired and bearded, with the clothing and stance and look of the philosophers. Over time, Christ as a shaggy-haired philosopher/teacher becomes the trajectory.[3] But always it is clear by the artistic representations that Christians understood Jesus as a philosopher.

As Christianity spread to the cities of the Roman Empire and moved out of the hidden art in the catacombs into statues, paintings, and sarcophagi in churches, Jesus is also depicted as a king and the emperor of the world. In paintings and mosaics, Jesus is in his risen state, seated and reigning over the world, scepter and crown in place, attended by angels and the saints.

While these two images of king and philosopher are distinct, they are not contradictory. For a large part of the philosophical tradition, stemming from Plato's *Republic*, the philosopher was the king, and a king must be a philosopher, a wise man. This has a strong tradition in the Old Testament too, with the first son of David, King Solomon, renowned as a wise-man king. The distinct images of Jesus as itinerant disciple-making teacher and as reigning emperor are not odd companions. They are juxtaposed to explain the one Jesus, philosopher and king.

One example of this important combination of images can be seen on a beautiful painted sarcophagus from around AD 300 called the Junius Bassus. We see Jesus going about his healing activities clad in a mantle and holding a scroll as an invitation to viewers to read what he taught—clearly a philosopher. On the same sarcophagus Jesus is also depicted as a god-king seated on his throne, ruling and reigning. These images are to be taken blended together to understand who Jesus is. As Taylor describes it, "Christ gloriously enthroned as a divinity *is* the philosopher-healer Christ."[4] Or as Tolkien said it earlier, "*The hands of the king are the hands of a healer. And so the* rightful king could ever be known."[5]

○○○○

58

We began this book with the third-century house church at Dura-Europos and its depictions of Jesus as a philosopher. We also met Justin "Philosopher" Martyr. Justin wasn't alone in thinking of Jesus as a philosopher. John Chrysostom, the fourth-century archbishop of Constantinople, regularly spoke of Jesus in the same way, saying that Jesus offered to the world the true *politeia* or way of structuring society and relationships, the philosopher par excellence. Augustine begins his discussion of Christian ethics by addressing head-on the great philosophical question of happiness, and he goes on to argue that Jesus provides the true answer.

But what about the New Testament itself? Is this widespread early interpretation of Jesus as a philosopher a deviation from the New Testament, or is it in fact rooted in the Bible? We've already seen that the Old Testament can be rightly read as a piece of ancient philosophy, trafficking in the same ideas and answering the same questions—the great human questions of knowing, happiness, ethics, and nature. The New Testament is the same. We only need to learn to ask of the New Testament writings another set of questions that we've unlearned to ask—the ancient philosophical ones.

○ ○ ○ ○

Even though he is one of the most famous people in the history of the world and the implications of his teachings are still being explored and written about and taught, he never wrote down anything himself. Of course, I'm talking about Socrates. I'm also talking about Jesus. To understand what the Gospels are, it is helpful to think about the kind of Greek literary and cultural context the Gospels were a part of.

Even though Socrates never wrote anything, he is well known and influential because the stories of how he lived, what he taught, and how he died were written down by his disciples.

Plato, who became a famous philosopher himself, was a disciple of Socrates and the main source of what we know about him. Plato reflected on the life and teachings of Socrates as he made his own disciples, setting up the famous Academy in Athens.

Plato was not alone in this habit of writing down the sayings and deeds of his teacher. In the ancient Greek and Roman worlds one of the most important and influential types of writing was the *bios*, the retelling of the "life" of someone famous. These *bioi* (pronounced "by-oi") were written about all manner of people—generals, emperors, heroes—but especially important were the biographies about the philosophers, because people needed help to figure out how to live well.

This habit of *bios* writing was firmly established by the time of Jesus and had proven to be a very efficient and effective way to present a philosopher's teaching, manner of life, and, especially important, the way in which the person died with dignity. This is the first clue that the Gospels are presenting Jesus as a philosopher: simply, the form and content of the Gospels very closely resemble the many *Lives* that were written about other ancient philosophers. And this is not something that only modern scholars have observed looking backward. This connection between the Gospels and the biographies of philosophers was universally assumed in the early church. Good old Justin the Philosopher/Martyr described what church services looked like around AD 150. Central to these early Christian gatherings, Justin tells us, was the reading aloud from the "memoirs" about Jesus, referring to the Gospels in the same way that the lives of the philosophers were described.

Why did people write a biography of a philosopher or a Gospel biography of Jesus? The reason was very clear—a biography was the most powerful and effective way to accomplish several things:

- to record the teachings and sayings of a wise man;
- to show stories that reveal the great person's character; and, bringing these together,
- to encourage people to become *disciples* of the philosopher by learning how to see the world in a certain way and how to behave in the world in certain ways.

The wise man whose life was recorded in the biography was both a conduit of truth and an example to be followed. A philosopher was only worth his salt if he actually practiced and modeled what he taught. As Seneca said, a teacher who is not an experienced model "cannot benefit me any more than a seasick pilot in a hurricane. . . . What help can a ship's sternman give me who is stupefied and throwing up?"[6]

A biography is the perfect means by which to accomplish the task of disciple making. A *bios* alone can simultaneously give content *and* the motivation of showing the teacher as an example. Abstract teachings divorced from a real, lived life would be as motivating and trustworthy as an obese exercise instructor or a bankrupt financial planner.

○ ○ ○ ○

The writing of biographical Gospels is our first hint that the New Testament authors were intentionally depicting Jesus as a philosopher. When we open the pages of the Gospels, we also see that the style with which Jesus taught shows striking parallel to the philosophers of his day. This can be seen in Jesus's teaching with aphorisms and parables.

An "aphorism" is a short, pithy saying that gives a memorable hook for how to see the world in a certain way. Often an aphorism is unexpected—that is, it has a twist in it that arrests and shocks the hearer into a great awareness of how to live life. Aphorisms are the regular tools of ancient wisdom teachers (philosophers) because of their long-lasting and life-changing effect.

Amor fati (the love of fate) is an easily memorized aphorism from the influential philosophy of the Stoics. It describes a way of seeing and being in the world that teaches that to be happy we need to embrace all that we experience, not longing for something else, some other fate. This is at the heart of the Stoic philosophy. If a person becomes a Stoic disciple, one can eventually learn to love what fate gives them. The aphorism *amor fati* provides a succinct, memorable saying that shapes those who meditate on it and incorporate its truth into their life experiences.

Think of how many heart-challenging and life-shaping aphorisms Jesus used. "The last will be first, and the first will be last" (Matt. 20:16). "What goes into someone's mouth does not defile them, but what comes out of their mouth, that is what defiles them" (Matt. 15:11). "Do not store up for yourself treasures on earth, where moths and vermin destroy, and where thieves break in and steal. But store up for yourselves treasures in heaven" (Matt. 6:19–20). And that's just a few. This is the kind of memorable teaching style that was the mark of ancient wisdom teachers.

So too with Jesus's famous parables. It has been estimated that at least 35 percent of Jesus's teaching in the Gospels is parabolic in form. We can count over sixty different parables that Jesus used. He was known for this style of teaching, and many of his parables are so famous that even non-Christians are familiar with them and can reference them by name—parables such as the prodigal son, and the lost sheep, and the sheep and the goats.

What many people today may not realize, including Christians, is that Jesus was not alone in his style of teaching with parables. In fact, this was a common technique that ancient philosophers used as a tool of their trade. Parables are powerful because they are imaginative and memorable and teach disciples to see the world in an unexpected way and invite an appropriate response in attitude and behavior—exactly what sages were all about. Aesop's fables are good examples of ancient wisdom parables outside of the Bible.

Jesus plays the role of a prophetic philosopher, a sage-prophet who is inviting people to see the world from the perspective of divine revelation that goes beyond human-centered knowledge. This prophetic emphasis does not make Jesus any less of a philosopher, but it does add an urgent edge to his teaching. Jesus regularly inserts the weighty tagline "He who has ears to hear, let him hear!" That is, "If you can understand my wisdom, then pay attention!" Jesus's teaching in aphorisms and parables would have immediately identified him as a philosopher during his own lifetime.

Another way Jesus functions as a philosopher is the many stories in which he is shown to be a winsome and powerful reasoner, especially in debates with other intellectual leaders.[7] For example, in Matthew 12:1–14 Jesus is challenged by the Pharisees and scribes about an issue that was very important to Jews—the keeping of the Sabbath. Jesus and his disciples appear to break the Sabbath laws. When he is questioned on this, Jesus engages in a nuanced set of reasoned arguments as to why in fact he and his disciples are practicing the Good (in biblical parlance, "righteousness"), while his opponents are not.

Jesus provides quick-witted arguments about how sometimes it was necessary to do actions that on the surface violated Sabbath laws but did not actually constitute lawbreaking. He uses a story from David's life and the practices of the priests. Jesus also reasons with his opponents by using practical illustrations from real life. For example, What do you do when your donkey falls into a ditch on the Sabbath? You get the animal out! Even though this involves work, it is an act of compassion that means that the Sabbath law has not been broken.

All of this is wisdom. It is the work of a philosopher, a sage. Reasoning through complex ethical issues, complete with memorable examples from life, shows Jesus to be remarkably wise and playing well the role of the philosopher. Many other examples from Jesus's life could be added. The *Greatest Hits* album of Jesus as a wise reasoner would include one of his most memorable aphorisms—when asked about paying taxes, Jesus quips, "Give back to Caesar what is Caesar's, and to God what is God's" (Matt. 22:21). With such philosophical acumen, Jesus is presented as winning every argument he gets dragged into.

○ ○ ○ ○

Another way Jesus is presented as a philosopher is through the summary of his teachings into philosophical epitomes. We use the English word "epitome" today to refer to a summary of the essence of something. In the ancient world an "epitome" had a similar sense, but one that was more specific and technical—it referred to a collection of a philosopher's teachings on a certain topic. A philosophical epitome was a memorizable group of sayings, usually organized around a big idea. It was not a comprehensive summary of the philosopher's teachings but a shorthand guide with the intention of helping disciples-in-training learn the master's way of seeing and being in the world.

When we look at the Gospels, we see that the Gospel writers utilize this common method to present Jesus's teachings. This is most apparent in the Gospel of Matthew. In Matthew, Jesus is presented as a disciple-making wisdom teacher (a philosopher) whose teachings are collected into five major topical epitomes (Matt 5–7; 10; 13; 18; 23–25). Jesus says and does many things outside of these teaching blocks, but these five collections provide the backbone to the organization of the whole

First Gospel. It would have been obvious to any first-century reader of Matthew that Jesus's teachings are skillfully arranged and presented as philosophical epitomes with the goal of making the Gospel of Matthew a powerful disciple-making book.

Not only is Jesus's mode of teaching akin to those of all other ancient philosophers, so too were the topics that he addressed in his teaching. *What* Jesus taught was not identical to other ancient philosophers—Jesus's own answers to the great philosophical questions of the day managed to offend both Jews and gentiles—but the topics and questions that were common throughout ancient philosophy were the same topics and questions that Jesus addressed.

The first epitome in Matthew, the Sermon on the Mount (Matt. 5–7), is a prime example. The sermon begins with nine macarisms (5:3–12)—nine statements concerning what it means to be truly and fully happy, to experience fullness of life and flourishing.[8] Whatever a philosopher proclaimed was *makarios* ("happiness, flourishing") revealed much about their whole philosophical system. Statements of *makarios* were very important for disciples to take note of if they were going to adopt their teacher's mode of life. It is no mere accident, then, that the very first teaching in the very first Gospel shows Jesus to be giving his own authoritative opinion on what constitutes true happiness. This is what philosophers did. The way of life that Jesus describes as being truly flourishing—poverty of spirit, lowliness, giving up one's rights, being wrongly persecuted—is shocking to any hearer in the ancient world or today. But what does not surprise first-century readers is that Jesus the Philosopher is pontificating on what makes for happiness.

The Sermon on the Mount goes on to present Jesus's epitome on what it means to be truly good. "The Good" (in biblical terms, "righteousness") was the focus of ancient ethics, and Jesus addresses it directly with his own authoritative vision.

Matthew 5:17–7:12 focuses on true righteousness. That is, what is the Good, and how does one live rightly in accordance with it? According to Jesus, the Good is found by looking at God himself, who is *teleios* (whole, mature, complete, perfect; 5:48).

Therefore, to be good/righteous requires seeing and being in the world in ways that match how God the Father himself is. This means obeying God's commands not just externally but from the heart, in the inner person (Matt. 5:21–48). This means performing acts of piety not for the praise of others but to receive a true and lasting reward from God himself (6:1–21). This means living in such a way that money and possessions don't consume and control you (6:19–34). This means treating others wisely and kindly, with the memorable guide being the Golden Rule—treating others as you would want to be treated (7:1–12).

Jesus himself is the ultimate model of all of this righteousness because he is the fully pleasing, Spirit-indwelt Son of God (Matt. 3:17). Jesus teaches about this greater righteousness so that his disciples have a vision to guide their lives in his ways. There is also a great urgency to Jesus's call to living in accord with the Good. The kingdom of heaven is at hand, bringing a change in the cosmos through Jesus (4:2). But not everyone will enter into this coming heavenly kingdom—only those who listen to and do the will of the heavenly Father (7:21; 12:50). Unless a person's alignment with the Good as revealed by Jesus is greater than the kind of righteousness that was being practiced by the scribes and religious leaders, they will not enter into the Father's coming kingdom. This added note of urgency makes Jesus the Philosopher's teachings even more powerful and effective in creating both disciples and enemies.

Verse after verse in the sermon, Jesus is not only presented as a great philosopher addressing the Good but also shown to be a law-giving, wise king. Jesus's message is about the coming kingdom of heaven in which he will be the king, authoritatively giving laws and interpretations of laws so that people might experience flourishing. This dovetails well with Plato's vision of what it means to be a philosopher-king, a vision that had already gathered into its stream Moses and Solomon. As the scholar Robert Kinney notes, the Sermon on the Mount "is not only successful in presenting Jesus as an authoritative mediator of both law and heavenly reward for those who follow his exhortations to righteousness; it is also successful in presenting Jesus as a Socratic figure—one who gathers disciples, teaches disciples, and so mediates their development for *the good*."[9]

The repeated presentation of Jesus as a sage culminates in the image Jesus uses to conclude the sermon—the contrast between wise and foolish builders (Matt. 7:24–27). The final call of the sermon is for people to listen to what Jesus has said and to *do* what he has taught—that is, to put into practice a life of discipleship based on his way of seeing and being in the world. Those who do not do what Jesus teaches are compared to a fool, a person who makes a wreck of their life by living in an unexamined and undirected way. By sharp contrast, the one who listens to Jesus and practices what he teaches is described as wise—a *phronimos* person. This loaded term is the same one the Greek philosophers used to identify those who practiced the ways of the philosophers.

○ ○ ○ ○

This representation of Jesus as a philosopher has been drawn mostly from the Gospel of Matthew, but this vision is not unique to Matthew. We could also foray into the Fourth Gospel, John's biography of Jesus. The most distinctive aspect of John's Gospel is the lengthy and profound dialogues that occur between Jesus and various people. Jesus converses with the Pharisee Nicodemus (John 3:1–15), the Samaritan woman he met at a well (4:1–26), various Jewish leaders (7:14–36), and even the Roman governor Pilate (18:28–40). In each conversation the issues are the big life-philosophical questions: How do we know things? What is the proper way and place to worship? And ultimately (with Pilate playing the role of a Cynic philosopher), "What is truth?" (18:38).

Throughout John's Gospel, the greatest repeated theme is life—how to experience the fullness and goodness of living well forever ("eternal life"). Jesus declares that the reason he came was so that people might experience fullness of life (John 10:10), the same promise that any good philosopher would offer. In fact, many scholars have noted how John's emphasis on "life" makes his the Gospel that is most obviously trying to present Jesus as a contemporary (and superior) philosopher in his day.

While the other Gospels also occasionally present Jesus as talking about "life" and "eternal life," Matthew, Mark, and Luke primarily describe Jesus's message as about "the kingdom of God." For the Jewish people, "kingdom of God" and "life" referred to the same thing. To enter into and be a part of God's kingdom means one will enter into a life that is full and flourishing—shalom. And conversely, to enter into fullness of life is to enter and live under God's good and perfect rule with his people. Thus, all the Gospels are presenting Jesus as the true teacher of life, the authoritative one who is "the way and the truth and the life" (John 14:6). The Gospel of John shows great sensitivity to the Greco-Roman context by describing Jesus's ministry primarily with the common philosophical language of "life" and only rarely with the more politically loaded verbiage of the "kingdom."

When we reread the Gospels sensitive to their historical and cultural context—a context that was rich with philosophers and philosophical life questions—Jesus makes sense as a philosopher.

○ ○ ○ ○

What about the rest of the New Testament? When we read the other parts of the New Testament we find that once again, the other twenty-three books are naturally and consciously interacting with the Greco-Roman philosophical world into which Christianity has arrived. What the Good is and how to live according to it drives the letters and treatises and vision of the rest of the New Testament. As with the Hebrew Scriptures, we can see this by examining the four compass points or main ideas that philosophy trades in—metaphysics, epistemology, ethics, and politics. (We'll save the discussion of politics for a later chapter.)

Metaphysics. As a reminder, metaphysics deals with the big questions of being, time, and nature. Metaphysical discussion is important because a philosophy is really not a philosophy at all if it doesn't have some reflection on the nature of the world we inhabit. This is because the universal idea is that to live well, to experience the Good, requires living in accordance with how things really are. We might describe this as cutting "with the grain" of the wood of the universe. Anyone who has run a jigsaw or circular saw through a two-by-six knows how different cutting with the grain and cutting against it feels. So too with life, according to the ancient philosophers. Only when we live in the direction of how things really are will we find peace and flourishing. So every philosophy has a series of metaphysical ideas, because all subsequent exhortations regarding ethics and politics are rooted in the great reality of the world. The New Testament is no different, and the grain with which we must cut is God himself.

Like every other aspect of the New Testament's teaching, the metaphysics of the New Testament are rooted in the same fundamental world-understanding as the Hebrew

Scriptures—namely, the belief that the eternal, timeless, singular God created humanity, male and female, as fundamentally good, with authority and responsibility over creation. God is in control of the world and is personal. He engages humanity graciously, even though there has been a breaking of this relationship because of sin. This world is bound in time, but God is eternal and will bring this current age to an end. He will reestablish his relationship with all of creation in a new and everlasting age of goodness.

The New Testament's vision is the same, but it adds key information that affects the interpretation of the whole. Crucially, the agent of God's creating and sustaining of the world is the Son of God, who became a real human, died, and was raised from the dead and ascended to rule over the world—that is, Jesus. This could not be said any more clearly than it is in the first chapter of Paul's letter to the churches in Colossae: "The Son is the image of the invisible God, the firstborn over all creation. For in him all things were created: things in heaven and on earth, visible and invisible, whether thrones or powers or rulers or authorities; all things have been created through him and for him. He is before all things, and in him all things hold together" (Col. 1:15–17).

It is hard to imagine a loftier claim than this! Thus, at the center of Christianity's metaphysic is the belief that a divine-human man, Jesus the Christ, is the manifest image of God himself. This world that we experience is actually created and upheld by the incarnated and now-risen Jesus, in unity with God the Father. This is a radical metaphysical claim not only for Jews but also for Greeks and Romans, who also had a highly developed metaphysic of both the cosmos and humanity's place in it.

For Greeks, the organizing structure of the world, the blueprint and pattern of how things came into being and hold together, was called the *logos*. It is no mere coincidence, then, that the Gospel of John opens with equally lofty claims about Jesus as the cocreator of the world and calls him the Logos (John 1:1). This beautifully and powerfully reorients the cosmological understanding of both Judaism and the Greek world. Jews did not expect that God would incarnate himself in his Son. Greeks did not expect that the logos could ever be called a person. This is a radical metaphysic. This claim about the nature of reality as centered in Jesus Christ will prove to be fundamental to Christianity's self-understanding. It becomes the basis for Christianity's claim to be the true story of the whole world—not just one religion or philosophy among many.

Another aspect of the New Testament's metaphysical discussion concerns time and the future. Sharing the worldview of the Hebrew Scriptures, the New Testament understands the universe not in an endless state of reincarnation or fluctuation between various forces. Rather, the world as we know it is a God-controlled temporary stage between its original created state and a new age to come. History is not circular but linear, heading toward a restoration of what was lost, a restoration that will even supersede the goodness of the original creation. Yet again, in a reinterpretation of the worldview of the Old Testament, the New Testament claims that Jesus is the means by which this new age is coming into the world. This can also be called the kingdom of God, when Jesus will be fully installed as the Sage-King, the good Ruler who will bringing flourishing and shalom to all of God's people.

Such ideas, which are crucial to Christianity, are philosophical claims. These bold statements about the nature of the cosmos, humanity, and time are foundational to Christianity's way of seeing and being in the world. They are consciously standing in a lively interaction with contemporary metaphysical claims.

○ ○ ○ ○

Epistemology. Epistemology deals with the question of how we know things and know them truly. Students of the Bible often wrestle with the question of what theme holds all of the Scriptures together. Some good offerings on the table are the glory of God, covenants, kingdom, and faith. Another good candidate for a whole-Bible understanding is the grand theme of knowledge. We've already seen in the Old Testament that, beginning with the Genesis stories of the creation and the fall, knowledge was key to what it meant for humans to live well. True knowledge of God was the key to life. Israel's fate rose and fell based on how well they knew the Lord.

The New Testament continues the biblical emphasis on knowledge—both the necessity of knowing God and the epistemological question of *how* we know. True knowledge of God is now found only through Jesus Christ, who perfectly reveals the *mystery* of God. That is, up until now the knowledge of God, the seeing of God clearly, has been limited and partial. Now that Jesus has come, all of the world has the ability to see and know God when they look to the perfect image enfleshed in the God-man Jesus. Jesus explains the Father to us (John 1:18).

There is still one problem with knowing, however, and this gets us to the great epistemological discussion of the New Testament. That problem is the same one that the Old Testament highlights and that started the whole problem of knowing: sin. Sin, the inherent and active resistance to God that is in all of humanity, affects not only behavior but also the mind itself—the capacity to reason consistently and humbly in pursuit of the Good. We call this the noetic effect of sin. Sin is knowledge-skewing. It obscures our ability to see the Good.

This noetic effect of sin can be seen in many places in the New Testament's teachings, but no place so clearly and foundationally as in Paul's great letter to the churches in Rome. In Romans 1 Paul begins his powerful theological treatise with an argument that isn't exactly what we'd expect. Paul starts on the very negative note that all people have a worship problem.[10] Human sin, Paul says, is a function of worshiping the wrong things. Instead of giving the uncreated God the highest honor and thanksgiving, humans have instead praised created things, thereby dishonoring God. This would be like obsessively kissing, praying to, and pampering a statue instead of speaking with, loving, and befriending a kind and wonderful person in the same room.

This misappropriated worship comes from a failure to know correctly and results in a greater darkening of our understanding. God gives humanity over to more of its own willful misunderstanding and misworshiping as a just judgment, resulting in further misunderstanding and misworshiping in a vicious downward cycle. This is humanity's choice and fate. Thus, sin is a matter of knowledge and an epistemological problem.

What is the solution to this dire state? The knowledge of God the Father revealed in God the Son is only accessible through God the Spirit. It is the Holy Spirit who quickens, awakens, and enlivens the mind—that is, enables our understanding. The solution to our Romans 1 sin-worship-knowing problem is found in Romans 12: "I urge you, brothers and sisters, in view of God's mercy, to offer your bodies as a living sacrifice, holy and pleasing to God—this is your true and proper worship. Do not conform to the pattern of this world, but be transformed by the renewing of your mind. Then you will be able to test and approve what God's will is—his good, pleasing and perfect will" (12:1–2).

That is, our worship of God can only be restored as we are transformed by the regeneration of our thinking. This regeneration and renewal of our minds is, according to the rest of Scripture, the work of the Holy Spirit. The spirit of this world

(Satan) has blinded the minds of unbelievers (2 Cor. 4:4), but the Holy Spirit reveals the glory of Christ to believers (2 Cor. 3:18). It is the Holy Spirit who washes and renews us (Titus 3:5). This enables a new knowledge that results in right worship.

Much more could be said about the big theme of knowing in the New Testament, but the important point is that the New Testament authors are once again dealing with issues that are core philosophical questions. They are universal human questions. The New Testament authors, especially more educated ones like the apostle Paul, are very aware of the discussion whirling around them in culture and are offering a distinctly Christian understanding in response. On the important questions of epistemology, the New Testament presents itself as a distinct philosophy, with the key idea being the spiritual blindness of all people and the necessity of the Spirit of God to reveal the knowledge that is necessary for life—knowledge of Jesus Christ.

○○○○

Ethics. Ethics (or as the older Christian tradition calls it, "moral theology") deals with the rightness and wrongness of our actions. This may sound like a simple topic, but it quickly becomes very complicated and nuanced:

- What is the source of our knowledge of right and wrong?
- What do we do when commands and good actions conflict, like when more than one good can be done and we have to choose, or when doing good in one sense (hiding Jews from the Nazis) involves otherwise wrong actions (like lying and deceiving)?
- Does it matter how I feel when I do something good (or bad)? Do my motives make an action good or bad?
- Is it okay if I can benefit from doing good?

The questions of ethics are very important in both the Old and New Testaments because of the metaphysical belief that there is a singular God who is consistent in his actions and who calls people to be like him. As we saw when discussing Old Testament ethics, the moral theology of the Hebrew Scriptures are *imitative*. This means God's ethical demands are rooted not in some external law or random code but in God's own nature. Humans will only find life and flourishing when they imitate their Creator, when they learn to inhabit the world in the ways that accord with God's own nature, will, and coming kingdom.

Closely related, biblical ethics are *agentic*, meaning that we as moral agents matter, that who we are as people is significant— our understanding, our emotions, our motives, and our desires are wrapped up in what is right or wrong. We as human agents matter in the equation of morality, not just whether the action itself is good or bad objectively. If I help relieve the suffering of a child but do it grouchily, berating the child the whole time, or with great resentment, or for some opposite motive such as that people will perceive me as compassionate when I'm really not— these *ways* of performing the action (my agency) are part of the determination of whether my acting is right and good. This is true even if the external factual part of the helping is the same.

This *imitative* and *agentic* kind of ethic is called a *virtue* understanding and is the driving factor of the Greek and Roman philosophical systems as well as the Bible. Virtue ethics focuses not just on the external issues of right and wrong but on our interior person and our development to be a certain kind of people. In the Bible, this means becoming more like God himself.

Jesus's teachings in the Gospels clearly manifest this virtue vision of ethics. The Sermon on the Mount is one of the many places in the Gospels where Jesus is shown to be a wisdom teacher/ philosopher. Intimately related, at the core of the sermon is a virtue-focused ethics. Jesus's critique of the Pharisees is that they lack wholeness or integration (Matt. 5:48), because although they perform good deeds and obey God's laws, they lack something more important—a heart of love that is attuned to God and to others. Thus, even in the midst of their externally apparent righteousness (goodness), they are deficient in both imitative and agentic ways. This applies to Jesus's disciples then and today, with the key idea of the sermon summed up in the challenge—"Unless your righteousness surpasses that of the scribes and the teachers of the law [that is, it is interior not just exterior], you will certainly not enter into the kingdom of heaven" (5:20).

The apostles' writings are built on the foundation of Jesus's life, teaching, and example. So we will not be surprised to find that when we turn to Paul, for example, we find a comparable Christ-centered, kingdom-oriented ethics of virtue. Every teaching and sermon and letter from Paul contains beautiful proclamations about what Christ has done on behalf of humanity and theological explorations of what this means. And subsequently, every teaching and sermon and letter naturally concludes with an invitation and exhortation to inhabit the world in ways that accord with these truths. These exhortations are imitative and agentic.

Explicitly, several times we find Paul root his teachings in the foundation of imitation. Christians are to imitate their leaders (like Paul) as those leaders imitate Christ. "Follow my example, as I follow the example of Christ" (1 Cor. 11:1). Paul says it this way in his letter to the Philippians: "Join together in following my example, brothers and sisters, and just as you have us as a model, keep your eyes on those who live as we do" (Phil. 3:17). And in one of the most powerful and important texts in the New Testament, Paul describes Jesus's choice to humble himself even to the point of death as the imitative basis for how Christians must relate to one another in humility and self-sacrificial love (Phil. 2:1–11). Make my joy complete, Paul says, by being united in love and spirit, by adopting the same way of thinking and being as Jesus himself.

Another way the imitative and agentic nature of ethics appears is with the role of the Holy Spirit producing fruit in us (Gal. 5:16–26). Utilizing Jesus's frequent image of a tree bearing fruit according to its nature and its health (Matt. 7:15–20; Luke 6:43–45; John 15:1–8)—notice the imitative idea—Paul describes the work of the Holy Spirit in the believer's life as bearing the natural fruit in us that reflects God's own nature. Our sinful nature (described as "the flesh") wants to produce a different kind of life in us, but when we walk in step with God's Spirit—notice again the imitation, keeping up with the Spirit as we walk—the result is that we become a certain kind of people, manifesting externally an interior goodness of love, joy, peace, patience, kindness, goodness, faithfulness, gentleness, and self-control (Gal. 5:22). This is virtue.

We've been looking only at a selection from Paul, but the same virtue-ethic approach is found throughout the rest of the New Testament, a prime example being in Peter's first letter. First Peter contains a household code comparable to Paul's (1 Pet. 2:18–3:7), and Peter quotes the same crucial Old Testament text that lies at the core of the Bible's imitative ethic—"Be holy, because I am holy" (1 Pet. 1:15–16; Lev. 11:44–45; 19:2). Additionally, Peter's primary exhortation to his Christian readers is that they base their lives of wholehearted righteousness on the example of Jesus himself. Christians are to imitate Jesus in their relationships with each other and with those outside the church with humility and mercy, even as Jesus himself did (1 Pet. 2:21–25).

○○○○

The purpose of the New Testament's ethical teachings, like those of its contemporary philosophy, can be summed up with one goal: to help humans come into fullness of maturity, to enter into what it means to be fully human. Christianity is offering the answer to what it means to mature into the fullness of humanity, with Jesus as the prototype of the new humanity, the Second and Perfect Adam.

This new-humanity emphasis can be seen in many places in the New Testament. At the end of the lengthy 1 Corinthians, which addresses a wide range of ethical problems in the church, Paul concludes with a list of aphorisms: "Be on your guard; stand firm in the faith; be courageous; be strong. Do everything in love" (1 Cor. 16:13–14). This translation inevitably covers up an important philosophical idea that is difficult to translate. The "be courageous" phrase is one word in Greek—an important word, *andrizesthe*, "be a man; act like a man." "Be courageous" is a better translation today than "be a man," because to today's English ear this sounds like bravado and chauvinism. If someone told someone else today to "act like a man," this would sound negative and degrading both to the male in question and to all women, who are implicitly denigrated.

But this is not what *andrizesthe* would have sounded like to Paul's hearers. Rather, this word taps into the widespread Greek idea that there was a standard of virtue that is honorable for humans (male and female) to pursue. To "act like a man" meant to exercise maturity, moral courage, and virtue in doing what is right. This same notion is also expressed in Greek with the phrase *teleios anēr* (the mature or complete human). Living a complete life as a virtuous human is the only way to experience flourishing.

The Letter of James also casts a vision for the Christian becoming a *teleios anēr* (James 3:2) by learning virtues such as taming the tongue and enduring through trials (1:2–4). Likewise, Paul prays for his disciples that they will grow into maturity and unity in the faith through knowledge of Christ so that they may become an *andros teleios* (complete man), which he then describes as the "whole measure of the fullness of Christ" (Eph. 4:13).

○ ○ ○ ○

Once again, these are all topics in Greco-Roman philosophy, which likewise teaches ethics for the purpose of bringing people into the fullness of humanity and maturity. We can see again that the New Testament's ethical teaching is trafficking in Roman- and Greek-understandable ways—that we need to become complete humans. The Christian difference is not the goal but the means. This is only possible, according to the New Testament, through the birth, life, model, teaching, death, resurrection, and ascension of the God-man Jesus, who gives the Holy Spirit to those who believe. The New Testament is a book of philosophy.

EDUCATING
EMOTIONS

A Big Emotional Debate

I n George Saunders's fascinating story "Escape from Spider-head,"[1] Jeff is a criminal in a not-so-distant future who killed a friend in an act of sudden rage. His sentence is lightened through his agreement to live in a scientific research facility. The lead researcher, Abnesti, sits in the control center, guiding the prisoners through experiments in the various room-arms jutting off from the middle like a spider's legs. Each prisoner has a "MobiPak™" surgically inserted into his or her back that can, at the touch of Abnesti's remote, inject assorted experimental drugs into their bloodstream. These drugs are at different stages of product development—some are known only by their research names (ED763; ED556), while others have already reached trademark status and become brands such as Verbaluce™ (a drug that enhances vocabulary and expressiveness by 80 percent) and Darkenfloxx™ (a chemical that causes unbearable sickness and pain). I won't attempt to rehearse the plot of the narrative, and reader be warned: the story is not for the faint of heart or sensitive spirit. But suffice it to say that the characters experience an expansive range of deep emotions—attraction, love, lust, peace, ambivalence, despair—that are all driven by and controlled through the chemicals administered by their MobiPaks™.

Saunders's stories always function on many levels. The dubious situation of prisoners legally "agreeing" before each drug is tested on them is subtly explored. The classic ethical "trolley problem" makes an appearance. But central to the premise of the story is the idea that our scientific command over biochemistry could come to the point where we (or at least the governments and corporations in charge) could completely manipulate people's emotional lives through precisely regulated drugs. Sexuality, aggression, purchasing interest—everything driven by emotions could be completely controllable through drugs.

○ ○ ○ ○

Emotions are a powerful and inescapable part of what it means to be human. Emotions are the mysterious energy that drives humans to love, kill, marry, divorce, buy things we can't afford, drink too much, and worship invisible deities. But what are they? According to the *Oxford English Dictionary* (*OED*), the French origins of our English word denoted civil unrest and public commotion coming from a mentally agitated state—"e" (out of) + "motion."

Like all bits of language, this word construes reality in a particular way. Our word "emotion," following the lead of the French origins, often occupies a semantic space that is negative and distinguished from rational thinking, as the *OED* goes on to define emotions: "strong feelings, passion; instinctive feeling as distinguished from reasoning or knowledge."[2]

The residential experts on our emotions today are not linguists but psychologists, neurologists, and therapists. What do they say? These doyens offer two competing answers on what emotions are. Some experts describe emotions purely neurologically and physiologically, as a function of body chemicals, like the experimenters in Saunders's story. What we describe as our emotions are really just perceived changes in our body, such as heart rate, breathing rate, and hormones that we then name with emotional terms.

Others, however, understand emotions psychologically, as a function of our mental expectations and outcomes. Happiness occurs when our experiences match our expectations, sadness when they do not. Anger comes when someone or something is perceived as blocking our desires and expectations. Emotions are a function of our mental state, our minds, not just our brains.

As theologian Kevin Vanhoozer astutely observes, theorists of emotions tend toward one kind of reductionism or the other, either reducing emotions upward (emotions are mental states) or downward (emotions are physical states).[3]

Who is right?

It's complicated. Our word "emotions" has come to occupy a mental space that brings more confusion than clarity. It is "too big for its britches," as my elderly mother would say. Or maybe better, "emotions" is too blunt of a tool to do the kind of exploratory surgery necessary to describe the human soul. Ancient philosophers and theologians made an important distinction—now lost—between "passions" (quasi-physical forces that move people) and "affections" ("thoughts of the heart" that affect the will).[4] Our singular word "emotion" now attempts to function in both of these distinct conceptual spaces, but it does so ineffectually. This modern conflation and confusion of the distinction between "passions" and "affections" will prove to be a problem, as we will see.

○ ○ ○ ○

Human emotions existed and affected life long before Freud and Prozac. The question of what emotions are and how to handle them is in fact an ancient one. Who were the experts on emotions in the ancient world? Who helped people understand what emotions are and how to manage them before there were neurologists and psychotherapists?

The answer is the ancient philosophers. Philosophers like Plato, Aristotle, Seneca, and Epictetus thought a lot about emotions and how to handle them. They recognized that our emotions drive what we do in life and underlie our actions, for good and for bad. Emotions were such a central part of the philosophers' life-shaping work that Martha Nussbaum summed up her lengthy description of Hellenistic philosophy with the title *The Therapy of Desire*.[5]

But that's not the whole story. These thoughtful philosophers also disagreed with one another on the fundamental question still debated today—What exactly *are* our emotions? The different ways the ancient philosophers answered that question were central to how they understood the world and were at the core of the whole-life philosophies they taught. All of this is relevant for our understanding of Jesus as the Great Philosopher.

○ ○ ○ ○

On one side of the emotions debate was Plato, who saw emotions (or "passions") as impulses that come upon us as an uncontrollable force.[6] Our souls have a rational and an irrational part, and the emotions come from the latter, illogical part. Plato famously describes the person as a charioteer who is driving two horses, one noble and good (reason) and the other badly bred and hard to control (passions).[7]

Plato's philosophical abstraction continued into ancient medical doctors like Galen (AD 129–200). Galen followed the sophisticated Greek medical theory of humorism, which taught that the human body consists of four basic fluids, or humors—blood, yellow bile, black bile, and phlegm. These four humors combined together differently in people to produce assorted temperaments (Latin for "mixtures"). Thus was born the first taxonomy of personality types—sanguine, choleric, melancholic, and phlegmatic. People's emotional lives were largely determined by various combinations of fluids in their makeup. According to this view, we have MobiPaks™ of four humors built right into us. Our emotions are not responsive to our minds and in fact battle against reason for domination. The methods of controlling emotions are not rational but aesthetic and bodily—reading poetry, listening to music, using rhythm.[8]

This noncognitive understanding of emotions continues on a long arc through history down to today. René Descartes (1596–1650) strengthened this conception by emphasizing that emotions or passions originate in the body, not the thinking soul (the mind). Echoing Plato, Descartes asserted that emotions are "animal spirits" in our blood that animate our bodies.[9] William James, the nineteenth-century philosopher and psychologist, modified Descartes's rationalist philosophy into a physiological psychology. The body experiences sensations (such as crying or the instinct to flee), which we then come to describe after the fact as emotions. The commitment to an evolutionary-biological metaphysic is woven throughout all of this—emotions are understood as learned physiological mechanisms rooted in survival techniques.

Many twentieth-century scientists followed in this line of thought, adding to the idea experimental studies showing the relationship between the body and emotions. Some psychological researchers, like Paul Ekman and Carroll Izard, particularly emphasize the body's influence on our perceived emotions. The use of our facial muscles, for example, affects our moods: Smiling produces greater happiness.[10] With advances in our ability to track what is happening in the brain, the height of this physiological understanding of emotions can be found in the field of neuroscience with bestselling authors like David Eagleman. In his books, such as *Incognito: The Secret Lives of the Brain* and *The Brain: The Story of You*, we see a reductionistic Platonic understanding wedded to the high-powered world of fMRI brain imaging. What is love? Brain chemicals. What drives someone to be a serial killer? Brain chemicals.

Even if one doesn't take an entirely chemical approach to emotions, today emotions are largely viewed as negative and the enemy of sound thinking. Pastor and author Marc Alan Schelske describes a little experiment he conducts with people in his seminars.[11] What would be your reaction if someone said to you, "You seem very reasonable today." Now how would you feel if someone said to you, "You seem very emotional today." Almost certainly you would receive the first sentence positively and the second not so much. To be described as reasonable is seen as good, while being described as emotional is bad. This distinction reveals a massive set of cultural values based in an unconscious anthropology of "reason = good" and "emotions = bad and dangerous."

And this is somewhat understandable. The uncontrolled passion of emotions can be a destructive force in our lives. A two-year-old's throw-self-on-the-ground-flailing behavior is not pleasant but is to be expected because of the emotional immaturity of a toddler. If a twenty-two-year-old, thirty-two-year-old, or fifty-two-year-old acts the same way, this lack of emotional control is deeply troubling and likely a sign of a mental health problem. Also, we often tell ourselves and others "not to make an emotional decision," meaning not to let emotions guide us more than reliable reason. Those of us who hold to certain ethical standards on marriage or money would rightly advise our teenagers that they need more than "It feels good" to justify their decisions about sex or stealing. This trains us to distrust and maybe even avoid emotions. When we take any or all of these negative experiences and add them to the reduction-ism of rationalism and brain-as-just-chemistry neuroscience, we have a recipe for a very negative evaluation of emotions.

○ ○ ○ ○

That's one approach. But it's not the only way to understand emotions today or in times past. An alternative conceptualiza-tion of emotions, what we can call a cognitive understanding, goes back to ancient philosophers as well. If Plato represents the emotions-as-noncognitive tradition, Aristotle stands as the progenitor of a different, integrated, cognitive approach.[12] Like his former mentor Plato, Aristotle understood that the soul has a rational and an irrational part, but rather than being distinct, these form a unity that makes us human. Not two bridled powerful horses, but one complex engine. Emotions are an example of this unity: We feel emotion in our bodies and souls *through* cognition, through using our minds in dialogue with our bodies. Emotions are the result of beliefs and judg-ments that we make. They are a cognitive evaluation, even if that evaluation is not always conscious, and even if that cogni-tive evaluation is sometimes wrong.

Thus, it is through our cognition, occurring at the speed of neurons, that when we are hungry, a sizzling steak induces the emotion of desire while a brick does not. The difference in these emotional responses is based on the cognitive judgments we make concerning the value of the different objects—in this instance, steaks or bricks for eating. This cognitive view of emotions also explains why one person, say a passionate vegan, would *not* feel desire for the steak but instead feel intense repul-sion that a slab of bloody flesh from an innocent animal has been cooked and served on a plate. (How do you feel about that description?) It is the *judgment* of the badness of meat that creates the very different emotional response.

89

And on the extreme end, we can imagine some odd psychological state where a person has become obsessed with eating bricks and subsequently *does* feel desire when sun-dried clay appears on a platter with accompanying cutlery of hammer and spoon. From a health perspective we would evaluate this cognitive judgment of the goodness of a brick diet as mistaken, but it is still a cognitive-emotional response. Pivoting in our reflections, if we were attempting to protect our windows against an approaching hurricane, being handed a pile of steaks would produce a very different emotion in us than if a pallet of bricks arrived. The emotions of elation, gratitude, and hope from obtaining bricks in that hurricane moment depend on the judgment or perception about what is needed. Emotions flow from and through our cognition.

Now it should be noted that Aristotle and subsequent thinkers understood that emotions can be irrational, based on faulty perceptions, and that mistaken emotions can cause self-deception and false judgments to be made. So the situation with our emotions is not simplistic and mechanistic, with appropriate emotions always following purely cognitive and rational processes. Additionally, our bodily sensations are involved as well. Different environments and activities—a quiet walk in the woods, the championship game of your city's beloved soccer team, a light snowfall on Christmas morning—affect our emotions. Despite these complicating factors, the way emotions function is primarily a matter of cognition—judgments based on the perceived value, goodness, desirability, or harmfulness of some person, situation, or object.

$$\circ \; \circ \; \circ \; \circ$$

The Greek philosophical traditions in many ways find their most mature and influential form in what is called the Hellenistic period, which ranged from the late fourth century BC until about the time of Jesus. Thanks to the expansive military success of Alexander the Great (whose tutor was none other than Aristotle), Greek philosophy and culture spread widely and took deep roots throughout the Mediterranean basin and beyond. When the upstart Romans eventually conquered, possessed, and expanded beyond Alexander's empire, much of the new Roman architecture and social structures were Latinized forms of their Greek predecessors. This included its philosophies. The great Roman philosophers like Seneca drew their inspiration from the Greek traditions that preceded them. The most popular and influential of these Hellenistic philosophies—Stoicism—promoted a cognitive view of emotions.

The Hellenistic philosophers, following the lead of their forebears Plato and Aristotle, cared very much about the flourishing of society, about promoting health and happiness. It was necessary, therefore, to teach people how to handle harmful emotions. Religion did not do this.

The problem with religion, the philosophers argued, was not so much the belief in gods per se, but the unbridled emphasis on emotion and passion that the belief in gods created. People lived in fear of the unpredictability of the gods, and the anger of the gods could be appeased only in noncognitive ways—through potions, spells, and mysterious rituals. Festivals associated with various deities were often debauched and uncontrolled events that were seen by the philosophers as harmful to society and to individuals.[13]

The philosophers' goal was to teach their adherents a way of life that would enable them to live with *ataraxia*, a tranquility of soul in all circumstances. Religion could not help this. *Ataraxia* was only possible through cognitive means, through learning to philosophize, through learning to educate our emotions. Philosophy teaches people to judge the world rightly so as to experience appropriate and manageable emotions. The scholar Martha Nussbaum says it this way: "The Hellenistic thinkers see the goal of philosophy as a transformation of the inner world of belief and desire through the use of rational argument. And within the inner world they focus above all on the emotions—on anger, fear, grief, love, pity, gratitude, and their many relatives and subspecies. . . . Emotions are not blind animal forces, but intelligent and discriminating parts of the personality, closely related to beliefs of a sort, and therefore responsive to cognitive modifications."[14]

The Epicureans (we'll discuss them a bit more later) and Stoics both talked a lot about emotions, but it is the Stoics who had the most to say and have had the longest impact. While following the basic cognitive approach to emotions they found in Aristotle, they also broke with the older Aristotelian tradition by emphasizing the necessity of a studied detachment from the world, including its emotions.

Apatheia (from which our word "apathy" eventually comes) was the key—don't let emotions control you at all. This is why we use the word "stoic" today to describe a nonemotional person. You may have seen the "Moods of Darth Vader" shirt where the same singular face of Lord Vader appears nine times, each with a different emotion listed under it—Excited, Angry, Sad, Frustrated, and so on. Someone could have made a killing selling a comparable "Moods of Seneca" toga in the first century.

While the Stoics' actual philosophy was more nuanced than our popular usage (see further discussion in the next chapter), this representation is not entirely inaccurate. Today's modern practitioners of Stoicism would be careful to point out that they aren't completely nonemotional, only that they have learned to control their emotional responses. Fair enough.

Nonetheless, the Stoics, much more than Aristotle, were suspicious of emotions because they believed that the key to happiness was a complete self-sufficiency that depended on no

Figure 6. Seneca the Younger (ca. 4 BC–AD 65) was a famous Stoic philosopher whose many letters and treatises are still influential today.

one and no circumstances. One's own cognitive-driven practice of virtue was sufficient for *eudaimonia* (happiness) according to the Stoics. By way of contrast, Aristotle maintained that *eudaimonia* depended on both virtue *and* fortune; circumstances do affect us.

For the Stoics, the issue of managing emotions was very important. If we open ourselves to any emotions, even positive

93

ones, we open ourselves to the negative passions as well. This means we are in danger of losing control. As Ludwig Edelstein describes it in his book *The Meaning of Stoicism*, "They are inclined to regard even the good passions as bad soldiers, bad allies in the fight of life, because one cannot rely on their leading us in the right direction."[15]

New Testament scholar Matthew Elliott highlights this contrast between Aristotle and the later Stoics through examining the emotion of anger. For Aristotle, it is right and appropriate to experience anger when atrocities are committed and injustice is done. For the Stoic, however, "it is not possible to have righteous anger without opening yourself up to the anger of revenge."[16] Therefore, for the Stoics, *ataraxia* and *eudaimonia* depend on learning to relate to the world in a detached way. But whether in the Aristotelian or Stoic approach, to live well requires philosophical reflection—learning to identify and analyze our emotions so that we can learn to educate them.

Even as the noncognitive Platonic tradition weaves its way in and out of intellectual fashion over the subsequent centuries, so too does the cognitive approach to emotions. Most of today's leading psychologists recognize the deep inner connection between our emotions, our cognition, and our bodies. Indeed, nearly every therapeutic counseling approach depends on the belief that behavior can at least partially be affected by cognitive processes—whether it be a classic Rogerian method or Emotion-Focused Therapy or, making it most explicit, Cognitive Behavioral Therapy. The best methods for psychological help will take into account the range of our complex lives—neurological, physiological, social, psychological, and relational. But all recognize that emotions can be educated.

○ ○ ○ ○

Philosophical reflection and psychological research have also shown that emotions are central to aspects of our lives that we may not immediately recognize—specifically, our ethics or morality. This was recognized in ancient philosophy and throughout premodern Christianity, but in the modern period it has largely been opposed or ignored. To state it most clearly: Emotions are central to our morality (1) in enabling us to determine what is right and wrong, and (2) as indicators of our moral character. Therefore, paying attention to and educating our emotions is crucial to the Good Life.

In the first instance, emotions play an important role in helping us determine what is moral and what is immoral. Feelings of justice, guilt, shame, and satisfaction at doing right are essential components that shape our ethics. As always with emotions, our feelings are not entirely trustworthy, because they can become distorted (for example, the false guilt or shame that victims of rape often feel; an absence of remorse in a serial killer). But emotions do represent judgments that we have about morality, even if those judgments are distorted. Thus, emotions (what we might call the mysterious conscience), when educated and formed well, are guides in helping us know what to do or not to do morally in a given situation. As Martha Nussbaum argues, it is not possible for us as humans to survey our moral choices in a detached, unemotional way: "In avoiding emotion, one avoids part of the truth."[17]

One bit of disturbing evidence for this comes from various experiments that have shown that people with injuries affecting the emotional centers of the brain are often unable to make ethical decisions and/or show a lack of moral inhibitions.[18] In his book *Descartes' Error: Emotion, Reason, and the Human Brain*, physician Antonio Damasio tells the story of his patient Elliot, whose whole life changed radically after successful brain surgery to remove a tumor.[19] He was healthy and his logical and reasoning skills were still in place; he still had a very high IQ. But due to damage to his frontal lobe, he lost all emotional capacity. The unexpected result was that he could no longer make any decisions; he was paralyzed by weighing the pros and cons of even trivial decisions such as how to sort his files. Without his emotional capacities, he could not figure out how to prioritize or weigh decisions of any sort. As a result, as Damasio concludes, "The cold-bloodedness of Elliot's reasoning prevented him from assigning different values to different options, and made his decision-making landscape hopelessly flat."[20]

In the past we would have called these abilities "reason," but an increasing number of studies show that reason only functions when it is paired with emotion. In their book *The Feeling Brain: The Biology and Psychology of Emotions*, Elizabeth Johnston and Leah Olson describe it this way: "Organisms are continually bombarded by a wealth of information—from outside and inside the body and brain—and emotions provide a way of evaluating and prioritizing what to respond to."[21]

The second part of our observation is that emotions not only affect but also *reveal* our moral character. This understanding is found at least as far back as Aristotle. Emotions are a vital part of a person's virtue or morality, because virtue requires an integration between all three parts of what makes us psychological humans—our reasoning, our emotions, and our behaviors. If any part of this triad is missing, virtue is lacking. To be virtuous, which is necessary for flourishing in the philosophical understanding, we must intentionally function as a whole (*teleios*) human. Only the wholeness between all the parts of our humanity enables life in its fullness—and this includes our emotions.

This means we cannot be virtuous accidentally. The virtue of courage is not at work, for example, if when fleeing a battle one drops his or her rifle and it discharges and kills the leader of the enemies. This behavior may result in a desired outcome, but no one would call this courage. Likewise, no one would describe a mean-spirited philanderer as having the virtues of justice, love, and mercy who writes a large donation check to a "Stop Human Trafficking" charity with money he has stolen. This lack of consistency between reasoning, actions, and emotions is the antithesis of virtue. And we would not describe a person as having the virtues of love and loyalty if their motives for kind deeds toward their spouse prove to be only for manipulative and self-serving reasons. Birthday flowers delivered from a wicked-hearted husband do not a virtue make. Motives, which are rooted in emotions (notice they come from the same root word), not merely thinking or behavior, play a crucial role in determining whether an action is virtuous.

We are just beginning to crack open an important way in which our emotional lives spread into the large realm of virtue and morality. In the modern period, in large part thanks to the ethical views of Immanuel Kant, emotions have been seen not as central to morality but as secondary and even problematic. Kant's nonvirtue approach to ethics emphasizes that right and wrong are a set of rational principles that are in no way connected to the character of the moral agent. Emotions are incidental at best and likely need to be made subservient. The noncognitive approach to emotions makes another (and particularly problematic) appearance.

But consider for a moment what our experience shows us. Emotions are in fact rightly an indication of one's moral character, and the agent's emotions are inextricable from the question of the rightness or wrongness of an action. If someone has joy in the suffering of another creature, say a kitten or a baby, we rightly describe this as wrong. Even if the person is not the behavioral cause of the suffering, a positive emotion while someone else is suffering is sadistic, not virtuous. Or if someone has embezzled or been unfaithful sexually to their spouse, the guilty person's emotional response—remorseful or indifferent—is a significant part of our evaluation of the person's character, not only in our gut instinct but also in legal sentencing. Similarly, a remorseless killer rightly receives a harsher sentence than a repentant one, and the original motive and emotion of the crime can make the difference between a conviction of manslaughter versus first- or second-degree murder. Emotions are part of one's character. This understanding of emotions was essential to ancient philosophers and to many modern philosophers as well.

○ ○ ○ ○

In sum, what we have seen about emotions is that they are not irrational impulses to be ignored or rejected. Rather, our emotions are deeply entwined with our cognition and our bodies. The best ancient philosophies and the best modern psychologies recognize this complex reality and advise us appropriately. Matthew Elliott describes the multifaceted and important role of our emotions this way: "Emotions are not primitive impulses to be controlled or ignored, but cognitive judgments or construals that tell us about ourselves and our world. In this understanding, destructive emotions can be changed, beneficial emotions can be cultivated, and emotions are a crucial part of morality."[22]

Christianity's Sophisticated Solution

During the night of July 31, 1976, a sudden storm dumped fourteen inches of precipitation in just a few short hours high up in the Colorado mountains. The accumulated rain had nowhere to go but down, and down the canyon of the Big Thompson River it went. This scenic, winding river became a torrent with a twenty-foot wall of water cascading through the valley at seventy miles per hour, taking with it exploding propane tanks, bridges, cars, branches, boulders, and people—people whose clothes were ripped off their bodies by the speed and severity of the flood. Nearly 150 of those camping and fishing in the canyon that night were drowned.

Among those in the valley was a group of thirty-five women leaders from Campus Crusade for Christ, including Vonette Bright, the wife of Bill Bright and cofounder of the international movement. These unsuspecting women were singing and praying when they heard the shrill state-trooper-megaphone calls to evacuate immediately. They piled into several cars and tried to flee the ranch. Some of the cars made it to higher ground by following the police, and the occupants were forced to scramble up onto the mountain to spend the dark night waiting. But in the blackness, two of the vehicles got separated and were swept off the bridge. A couple of the women in those cars made it out of the windows and tumbled down the river, mouths and noses and lungs stuffed with mud, debris, and rocks until miraculously both of them hit trees that they were able to climb and wait out the storm and the night. The others were lost—seven of the thirty-five women.

One of those who survived that traumatic night was Ney Bailey (along with Vonette Bright). As she struggled to process what had happened, she was overwhelmed with grief, fear, questions, and, undoubtedly, what today we would call survivor guilt. Her years of faith had also trained her in the habit of giving thanks. And in brokenhearted authenticity, along with thousands of other Crusade staff from all over the world, she offered praise and thanksgiving to her God, expressing trust in God's goodness and trustworthiness in all things.

And she wrote a book. To help her in her struggle against becoming bitter and cynical, Bailey honestly explored her range of emotions and put them down in writing to help others. That book, *Faith Is Not a Feeling*, is still in print more than forty years later.

Just over ten years after the Big Thompson River flood, I met Jesus through the witness of a Crusade staffer, who was part of the ongoing legacy of the faithfulness of the Campus Crusade organization. And shortly after that, as a passionate young man, brand new to the Christian faith and full of baggage and disordered emotions, I was given *Faith Is Not a Feeling* to read. And it helped. Ney Bailey's wisdom was not to ignore emotions, as the title might imply and which has been the source of some criticism. Rather, she emphasized that faith in God is *more* than our feelings—emotions that will inevitably range through positive, negative, and numb. Additionally, faith in God can bring us through debilitating and destructive emotions like bitterness into a place of joy and gratitude and peace.

○ ○ ○ ○

We have been discussing the central role that emotions have played and continue to play in a philosophy of life. What about the Bible and Christianity? If it is true, as I am arguing, that Christianity is offering a philosophy of life, that Christianity is thoughtfully addressing the great human questions and experiences, then it must be that Scripture has something important to say about emotions. If the Bible and Christianity ignored emotions altogether or presented a simplistic or patently wrong view of emotions, then it would not be worthy of the label of "whole-life philosophy." Have no fear (or any other negative emotion). When we turn to the Bible and ask whether it speaks to the question of emotions, we find that the answer is more than a generic yes. Emotions prove to be a large, nuanced, and practical area of discussion all throughout Scripture, as they are rightly part of what it means to live a Good Life. The Bible and Christianity have a remarkably sophisticated philosophy of emotions.

○ ○ ○ ○

To understand something complex and nuanced, it is often helpful to consider it in contrast to what is surrounding it. In sculpture, this is called relief (from the Latin verb *relevo*, "to raise"). Relief sculpture stands out from the surface it is carved out of and connected to, as opposed to a freestanding sculpture on a plinth.

Christianity's ornate and sophisticated philosophy of emotions stands in relief to its surroundings, both in the ancient world and today. To understand the Bible's approach to emotions, we will consider ways in which it is similar to and distinct from the philosophies of emotion on offer in the world.

First, the similarities. Christianity is a religion, meaning it deals with the divine and makes deep claims about the nature of reality, but it is also more than that. As a religion, Christianity

Figure 7. Angel sculpture on a plinth, Pont Sant'Angelo, Rome

Figure 8. Relief from the Arch of Titus, depicting the capture of the menorah from the Jerusalem temple

provides liturgies—customs and habits that shape the sensibilities of its believers and direct them to worship a Being outside of themselves. But recall that for the philosophers, especially at the high point of the Hellenistic period, this is precisely where the discussion of emotions is so important. Reasoned philosophy, not just religion, was crucial to living a good and peaceful life (*eudaimonia* and *ataraxia*). That is, unlike what the religions of the day had to offer, with their uncontrolled ecstatic emotional exuberance, the philosophers proposed a wisdom-loving way of thinking and living that could educate the emotions. The key to life was found in philosophy—a practiced learning to see and be in the world in certain ways.

So at first this would seem to mark a difference between Christianity and its contemporary philosophies. However, the key is to recognize that Christianity is not merely a religion, but is a religious philosophy. Like the philosophical traditions with which it is dialoguing (in relief), Christianity does *not* encourage ecstatic emotional practices like its contemporary religions. Rather, it considers the emotions as important but controllable by proper reasoning. Thus, within its religious metaphysic, Christianity presents itself as a philosophy that is aware of the importance of educating emotions.

Even with the church practices of speaking in other tongues and prophesying—what to outsiders would be classic dangerous religious exuberance—the New Testament is remarkably restrained. The apostle Paul addresses this directly, giving strong instructions about how to handle these Spirit-inspired utterances. Church services must be conducted with order and wisdom (1 Cor. 14:26–40). If not, outsiders will wrongly perceive that Christians have lost their minds (14:23). That is, without controlling emotional outbursts, people will wrongly suppose that Christianity is just another example of foolish religion. Instead, Christianity is an astute religious philosophy that exercises thoughtful restraint.

This leads to another crucial similarity between Christianity and its contemporary philosophies: Christianity's cognitive approach to emotions. Like the Aristotelian tradition and unlike the Platonic one, the Bible's view of emotions is not that they are irrational and bad, uncontrollable and dangerous. No, emotions are inextricably woven with our ethics, habits, understanding, and bodies—in short, what it means to be human. Emotions are part of life and are not to be avoided, but they must be educated through a thoughtful way of seeing the world.

Christianity is also similar to its surrounding philosophies in anthropological understanding; specifically, where emotions reside in us as humans—in the heart. Every language uses body parts as metaphors for something deeper. Various languages metaphorically place emotions in different parts of the body. In Greek, for example, compassion is found in the intestines. For Turks, love is in the liver.

The Bible regularly uses the metaphor of "heart," but not in the way that modern English does. In English, the heart metaphor is used primarily as a container for emotions, especially love. Our word "heart" today connotes emotions as opposed to reason. So "heart" can be laid side by side in contrast with "head"—emotions versus reason. This contributes to the conflation of "passions" and "affections" in how we use our word "emotions."

But the situation is very different for the Bible. In both Hebrew and Greek, the words that are translated into English as "heart" are broader and shaped differently. The Hebrew *leb* and the Greek *kardia* mean the inner person in comparison with the outer; the true person *as a thinking and feeling being* is what "heart" indicates. In this, Christianity's understanding of emotions overlaps significantly with its surrounding cultures—Jewish, Greek, and Roman. The true inner person includes both reason and emotion. We cannot fully separate head and heart.

○○○○

So we are beginning to see that, when examined in the cultural and intellectual context of its day, Christianity makes sense as a philosophy, addressing the central role that emotions play in a whole philosophy of life. But here is where the beautiful and striking relief sculpture that is Christianity stands out. There are substantial differences in the Bible's philosophy of emotions that reflect a distinct metaphysic.

What are the distinct aspects of the Christian philosophy of emotions?

First, the God of the Bible has emotions and he is thoroughly good. In Greek and Roman mythology, which had a lasting cultural impact even in the philosophical era, the gods were often seen as the source of fickle and bad emotions. On the contrary, the biblical understanding, in both the Old and New

Testaments, was that the true God also experiences emotions, but not in an uncontrolled way, and never capriciously; God is not ornery, tempting and messing with humans and their emotions. But neither is God emotionless.

In the Bible God is described as having emotions such as anger, jealousy, grief, joy, satisfaction, and, most of all, love.[1] Very often God is described as having and acting from real emotions. Out of a proper concern to not think of God's emotions in purely human terms, theologians have often emphasized God's "impassibility." You can see the word "passions" hidden in there, negated. The doctrine of impassibility means that God is not fickle and untrustworthy, because he does not change and shift. It means that it is impossible for God to succumb to passions out of his control. That's true and good (Num. 23:19; Mal. 3:6; James 1:17). But unfortunately, for many people in the modern period impassibility has come to mean that God is emotionless.[2]

Impassibility, however, should not be understood to mean God lacks emotions and that the many references to God's emotions should be written off as mere human projections onto him. This common approach to God's emotions reflects a Platonic and/or Stoic view of emotions as inherently bad and untrustworthy, a view that the Bible does not share. If one believes all emotions are bad, then obviously God cannot have them. But the problem is in that assumption. Emotions are part of reasoning and being human, and the fact that humans have them as part of our being made in the image of God (not just as part of our sinfulness) speaks positively to God's emotions.

The problem with human emotions is with the human part, not the emotions part. Humans, who are both limited and broken, have emotions that can necessarily be ill-formed, perverted, and disordered. God, who is incorruptible and perfectly whole, has emotions appropriately and perfectly. As one writer helpfully says, "Because God has an infinite mind, infinite power, and an infinite heart, emotions don't disrupt God's character. They don't move God to act in ways that are anything other than ultimately loving."[3]

If anyone is still hesitant to think of God as having emotions, we need only consider the clear testimony of the Gospels, which repeatedly show the incarnate Son of God, Jesus, as a fully emotional being. To be human is to have emotions, and that is a good thing, with Jesus as the ultimate model. John Calvin notes that "those who imagine that the son of God was exempt from human passions, do not truly and seriously acknowledge him to be a man."[4] But we need to go further and be clear that the emotions of Jesus are not only part of his being human but also reflections of the Triune God's own proper and full experience of emotions.

B. B. Warfield astutely observes that many Christians have tended to ignore or disregard Jesus's emotions because of the latent influence of the Stoics. Recall that the Stoics emphasized that the ideal state was one of *apatheia*, freedom from all emotions and a kind of detachment from the world.[5] This notion of perfection as freedom from emotion has lingered and haunted the Western mind ever since, causing us to miss the central role that emotions play in Jesus's own life and teaching.

Jesus wept (John 11:35). The significance of this two-word verse is not only that it is handy for kids who are required to memorize a Bible verse. More importantly, it is a glimpse into the emotional world of Jesus. Jesus wept, marveled, hoped, longed for certain things to happen, and lamented (Matt 8:10; 27:46; Luke 19:41; Heb. 12:2).

When we read the four Gospels with our receiver tuned in to the emotions frequency, we will see that of the many emotions ascribed to Jesus, there are three that occur most frequently. Jesus is first of all described as *compassionate*, as feeling loving pity and care for people. This motivates his countless days and nights of healing people and his ultimate work of giving his own life (Matt. 9:36; 14:14; Mark 1:41). Second most often, Jesus is shown to be *angry*—at compassionless people primarily, but also at injustice and consequences of the fall, like death (Mark 3:5; 11:15–19; John 11:38). Third, Jesus is shown to be joyful. He rejoices regularly, gives thanks joyfully in all circumstances, and instructs his disciples to do the same (Luke 10:21; John 15:11; 17:13).

A joyful Jesus is maybe the most unexpected picture we get of Jesus in the Gospels—unexpected because so much of sacred art throughout the centuries has pictured Jesus as dour and always serious. This is especially so in the Western tradition, which focused its theology and images on Jesus's suffering. Crucifixes become primary, and Western church architecture reinforces this with cathedrals built in the shape of a cross (as compared to

Figure 9. Dome mosaic from Sant'Apollinare in Classe

Figure 10. Altar with crucifix in the Cathedral of Ravenna

the octagonal basilica of the Eastern tradition, which primarily depicts Jesus as risen and blessing others). I remember being struck by this difference when visiting the various churches in Ravenna, Italy, some of which are ancient Eastern-style basilicas and others baroque-era Western-style churches.

In a class I teach on the Sermon on the Mount, I often show various film versions of Jesus's famous mountainside homily. There is one that unsettles many students. It's not the black-and-white, jarring offering from the Italian Marxist Pasolini. It's not the brilliant Claymation version. It's the film where Jesus is happy. In the *Visual Bible* version, Jesus delivers the Sermon on the Mount in a dialogical, loving, and engaging way, even laughing along with the crowd at some of the absurd images he uses, like the would-be plank-eyed surgeon (Matt. 7:3–5). This shocks us. We want our Jesuses to have nice British accents and not be very emotional, and especially not cheerful! So students are often taken aback at this happy Jesus.

But it is worth noting that in contrast with John the Baptist, Jesus was described as eating and drinking, and indeed was maligned as a glutton and wine-imbiber, a friend of publicans and sinners. He went to a lot of dinner parties. There is nothing to indicate he was habitually sorrowful, dour, and overly serious. After all, people—regular, nonreligious people—were very attracted to him. He must have been accessible, warm, and joyful.

Jesus was a real person and so experienced the many emotions that accompany our physical experiences, including negative ones—thirst, hunger, weariness, pleasure. Jesus wailed, raged, was agitated, and was openly joyful. His last moments included a wholehearted cry of despair (Matt. 27:46). As Warfield observes, "Nothing is lacking to make the impression strong that we have before us in Jesus a human being like ourselves."[6]

And at the same time we see in Jesus's humanity a picture of the complete human who reflects God's own image in a way that no sinful human has (Heb. 1:1–4). Jesus was fully emotional, but in a way that was always harmonious, not imbalanced, inappropriate, or disordered. Both compassion and indignation are joined together and exercised rightly. "Joy and sorrow meet in his heart and kiss each other."[7] Jesus's emotions are full and strong, not pale, but they never master him or function wrongly. In this the begotten Jesus images the Triune God's emotional life and also provides an imitative model for us, who are made in God's image but are broken and disordered. Emotions are good and necessary when educated.

○ ○ ○ ○

In addition to Ney Bailey's *Faith Is Not a Feeling*, another influential Campus Crusade teaching in my university days was the train illustration. Figure 11 depicts the *Schoolhouse Rock!*–era version of it that I was familiar with.

The point of this little image is this: Faith in the historical facts of God's love for us in Jesus is what drives our lives, while feelings may or may not follow along; emotions are not central to our Christian lives and certainly shouldn't be given the leading role.

This teaching from Crusade's little booklet on how to live "the Spirit-filled life"[8] can be interpreted positively or negatively.

Figure 11
Train illustration

Inspired by a Cru illustration

Positively, along with Bailey's *Faith Is Not a Feeling*, this Fact-Faith-Feeling model is beneficial in recognizing that we can't base our lives merely on the fickleness of emotions. Especially as a central teaching for university-attending eighteen-to-twenty-two-year-olds at such a crucial and emotionally tumultuous time (with not-yet-fully-developed frontal lobes and lots of sudden freedoms), this is to be commended as wise guidance. I know I needed it. Additionally, even though this is probably not what the designers were thinking, one could interpret this illustration in line with a cognitive approach to emotions—that emotions are primarily the result of, or subsequent to, cognitive judgments.

But on the negative side, this train illustration could be interpreted and applied as another unhelpful promoter of the negative-view-of-emotions tradition. By relegating emotions to a noncrucial role, as something that may or may not be there in our lives, as unrelated and nonessential compared to the "faith in the facts" engine, we may unwittingly fall back into this Platonic view of emotions. Many Christians have been taught to view emotions this way. This is a problem because this is patently *not* the view of the Bible and Christianity, as we have begun to see and will discuss more momentarily.

Even if we don't adopt a fully antiemotion view from the train illustration, many people, like I did, take away the sense that emotions are suspect and to be kept somewhat at bay, a kind of unarticulated Christianized Stoicism.

○○○○

There is another important way that Christianity's sophisticated view of emotions stands in relief to the surrounding philosophies of the day: the question of detachment.

We noted that around the same time as Jesus, Stoic philosophy was very widespread and influential—and understandably so. Stoicism was a very thoughtful whole-life philosophy that offered practical advice on how to live uprightly and find happiness. It had influential and virtuous advocates like Seneca and the later Roman emperor Marcus Aurelius.

Stoicism's answer to the great human question of happiness, which has remarkable similarities to its contemporary Buddhism farther east, is that one must learn to be detached from all circumstances and the emotions they evoke, both good and bad. Only this kind of studied detachment will enable one to find *ataraxia* and *eudaimonia* (tranquility and happiness).

In comparison to this very practical and often effective practice, the Christian philosophy of emotions shows remarkable refinement. Unlike with Stoicism, emotions are not to be disregarded, ignored, minimized, vilified, or placed in the "unimportant and untrustworthy" category. Quite the contrary. As we have already seen, God is described as having emotions, and Jesus models a full emotional life. Additionally, a full range of emotions is displayed by God's people throughout the whole Bible, and they are not condemned or written off as merely "emotional" for expressing their very human feelings. Indeed, the heart and center of the Old Testament is a book of songs (Psalms) that articulates and commends the emotional life. King David, the author of many such psalms, is one of the trifecta of most important people in the Old Testament (along with Abraham and Moses), and he was known for his deep passions and display of emotions (2 Sam. 6:5–16; 19:1–4).

Moreover, throughout the Old and New Testaments many emotions are explicitly commanded and commended:

- Rejoicing (Rom. 12:15; Phil. 3:1; 4:4)
- Having compassion (Zech. 7:9–10; Eph. 4:32; Col. 3:12; 1 Pet. 3:8)
- Being patient (Rom. 12:12; Eph. 4:2; 1 Cor. 13:4)

113

- Grieving and regretting (Joel 2:13; Acts 2:38; 2 Cor. 7:10)
- Fearing and not fearing (Isa. 41:10; Matt. 10:28)
- Loving (John 13:34–35; 15:12; Rom. 13:8; Col. 3:14; 1 Pet. 4:8; 1 John 4:7–10)

So to put it most simply: the Bible's view of emotions is cognitive but not Stoic; emotions are controllable, but detachment from emotions is not valued or good.

Yet here is where the nuance of the Christian philosophy comes into its fullness. While promoting the good of emotions, Christianity also recommends a measured and intentional detachment from the world and its circumstances for the sake of living a tranquil life. The apostle Paul, who experienced the heights of joy and passion (Phil. 1:18; Col. 1:24), also knew firsthand the depths of despair, pain, and grief (Rom. 9:2–4), even describing his emotional experience at one point as living with the feeling of a sentence of death hanging over everything he did (2 Cor. 1:8–9).

Yet, like a good philosopher, Paul also says that he has learned how to be content regardless of his circumstances and feelings. Writing to the Christians living in the Roman colony of Philippi, Paul gives several specific instructions regarding emotions. "*Rejoice* in the Lord always. I will say it again: *Rejoice*!" (Phil. 4:4); "*Do not be anxious* about anything, but in every situation, by prayer and petition, with thanksgiving, present your requests to God" (4:6).[9] The result of these cognitive-emotive choices will be the kind of peace that every soul longs for—a transcendent peace that comes from God himself (4:7). Emotions are part of what it means to be Christian.

But then Paul drops a line the great Stoic Seneca would be proud of: "I have learned to be content whatever the circumstances. I know what it is to be in need, and I know what it is to have plenty. I have learned the secret of being content in any and every situation, whether well fed or hungry, whether living in plenty or in want" (4:11–12).

So emotions matter, yet Christians must have a measured detachment from circumstances that would normally cause the range of emotions. That's a very nuanced position. How can one pull this off? The Stoic answer seems easier—just concentrate on detachment, because life is too unpredictable.

But Christianity is very clear on how one can walk this fine line of full emotions with measured detachment. The answer to this great human question is profoundly divine. And as always, the Christian understanding is rooted in the person of Christ. We don't have to wonder what the secret is. Paul tells us: "I can do all this through him [the risen Jesus] who gives me strength" (Phil. 4:13).

Paul got this transformative understanding from Jesus himself, both his teaching and his example. Jesus, not insensitive to the emotions of his disciples, instructs them to rejoice (an emotion) in the midst of persecution, suffering, and rejection (all emotions and emotion-evoking). How? Through the *knowledge* that such unjust suffering and emotional distress has been endured by God's faithful prophets in the past *and* through the sure hope that God will reward, restore, and recompense all those who have suffered on his behalf (Matt. 5:10–12). This is neither mindless emotional exuberance nor studied emotional detachment. It is a fully emotional life educated by knowledge and hope in God.

Jesus also models this himself in his darkest hour. With distress sufficient to produce drops of blood, even while his close friend was betraying him, knowing the anguished pain and shameful experiences he was about to endure, Jesus prayed (Matt. 26:36–46). His garden of Gethsemane prayer becomes the model of real emotions educated through faith and hope in God. "Not my will but your will be done" is the posture that manifests Jesus's practiced and wholehearted philosophy of emotions. He is fully present to his emotions, even painful ones, and yet finds peace through turning in trust to the divine Father.

○○○○

One of the strengths of Aristotle's cognitive view of emotions is that it accounts for the reality that emotions are integral to morality and ethics. The moral agent's emotions are both revealing of a person's character and a necessary part of what it means to be moral. Contrary to the view of ethics that has dominated in the modern period, morality is more than a set of right-and-wrong principles. The moral agent's virtue (including emotions) is a necessary part of ethics.

Unfortunately, Christian ethics in the modern period has often suffered from the Kantian missteps, especially in the Protestant tradition. Many Protestant ethicists have perpetuated a view of morality that is correct in emphasizing that morality is based on God's revelation but have missed the central role that the virtue of the moral agent plays. Failing to appreciate the Bible's nuanced philosophy of emotions has been one of the consequences of this ethical understanding, while at the same time it has also contributed to this insufficient ethical approach.

Central to Hebrew life is the Shema: "Hear, O Israel: The Lord our God, the Lord is one. Love the Lord your God with all your heart and with all your soul and with all your strength" (Deut. 6:4–5).

When Jesus is asked about what the greatest commandment in the Bible is, he answers with the Shema plus a crucial addendum:

"Teacher, which is the greatest commandment in the Law?"
  Jesus replied: "'Love the Lord your God with all your heart and with all your soul and with all your mind.' This is the first

and greatest commandment. And the second is like it: 'Love your neighbor as yourself.' All the Law and the Prophets hang on these two commandments." (Matt. 22:36–40)

Notice that this central biblical teaching is a command to have a certain emotion—specifically, love. Love is more than an emotion, but it is not less than one. Love is a way of seeing and being in the world that is rooted in the heart, which necessarily includes the emotions. God's people are regularly commanded to obey—to do certain actions and to avoid others. But undergirding all of these commands and arching over them all are the two greatest commandments, which focus on love. To do what is moral, to be ethical, requires obeying God with love, and this obedience focuses on the emotions of the person.

○ ○ ○ ○

Throughout the Gospels Jesus has sharp and repeated conflict with one group more than any other—the morally and religiously conservative "scribes and Pharisees." What is the source of Jesus's tension with this group? It is not their conservative view of the authority of Scripture or that their moral practices are all wrong. Jesus promotes many of the same views as the Pharisees regarding the sanctity of marriage and good practices such as fasting, prayer, giving to help the poor, and meditating on Scripture.

Jesus's pointed critique of the scribes and Pharisees is focused not primarily on their behavior but instead on an emotional failure, a moral breakdown at the level of their emotions. He calls them "hypocrites" not because they are living secretly immoral lives but because there is a disconnect between their otherwise good outward actions and their inner person, their hearts.

What is the scribes' and Pharisees' problem? It is cardial. It is emotional. When they see the needs and suffering of others, they lack compassion; they value strict adherence to external laws over love for those in need (Matt. 12:1–14; 15:1–9). When they pray, fast, and give money to help the poor, their motives (which are rooted in emotions) are disordered and misplaced; they love the praise of other humans over that of God (Matt. 6:1–21). When the Pharisees are full of anger, lust, or a desire for vengeance, it is the opposite of being righteous, even if no immoral outward actions are performed. To not murder is good, but real righteousness requires one not to be angry and hateful. To avoid adultery is good, but real righteousness requires one not to be driven by lust (Matt. 5:17–48). Anger and lust are emotions, not just actions. Righteousness includes emotions.

○ ○ ○ ○

That's the negative side of things. Christianity critiques any type of morality that ignores or dismisses the central role of emotions. But Christianity also speaks positively about the importance of emotions. In many New Testament texts, Christians are described in particular ways for the purpose of exhorting them toward certain practices and habits. Over and over again these descriptions direct our energies toward educating our emotions.

For example, take Paul's description of two possible human states—the Christian filled with God's Spirit versus the person left in a merely human state, "in the flesh." After quoting Jesus's command to "love your neighbor as yourself" (Gal. 5:14), Paul speaks about these two opposing realities in terms of their desires—the Spirit and the flesh have passions/emotions/desires that are contrary to each other (5:16–17). The subsequent description of those in the flesh includes a list of immoral practices, but not only practices—it also includes specific fleshly emotions (bolded): "The acts of the flesh are

118

obvious: sexual immorality, impurity and debauchery; idolatry and witchcraft; **hatred, discord, jealousy, fits of rage, selfish ambition, dissensions, factions** and **envy**; drunkenness, orgies, and the like" (5:19–20).

By way of contrast, the Spirit-filled person manifests an opposite set of emotional habits—both direct emotions and habits motivated by certain emotions, capped off with the summative description of self-control over emotions: "But the fruit of the Spirit is **love, joy, peace, forbearance**, kindness, goodness, faithfulness, gentleness and self-control. Against such things there is no law" (Gal. 5:22–23).

Paul's final description of the Spirit-filled Christian is appropriately summed up with a spiritual application of Jesus's own physical crucifixion, showing that the Christian is defined as the person who by the Spirit and union with Christ has gained control over these negative "fleshly" emotions: "Those who belong to Christ Jesus have crucified the flesh with its passions and desires" (Gal. 5:24).

So to be filled with the Spirit is to have certain emotions and to learn to control other ones.

○ ○ ○ ○

The Christian community is also often described in ways that reflect Christianity's philosophical commitment to educating our emotions. The fruit of the Spirit that we have just discussed are manifested in relationship to others. Other texts explicitly focus on the corporate life of Christians, and these are once again full of exhortations to avoid certain emotions and cultivate others.

Romans 12 is a good example. While discussing the different Spirit-gifts that God has given people for the building up of the church, Paul encourages people to use these gifts in certain emotion-sensitive ways—giving with a generous heart, leading with diligent care, and showing mercy toward others cheerfully (Rom. 12:8).

This leads Paul to his favorite topic, following Jesus's own lead—love. Notice once again how many particularly emotional traits are identified in this high-level description of church life (emotions are bolded; actions motivated by a certain emotion are italicized):

> **Love** must be **sincere**. **Hate** what is evil; *cling* to what is good. Be *devoted* to one another **in love**. *Honor* one another above yourselves. Never be lacking in **zeal**, but keep your **spiritual fervor**, *serving* the Lord. Be **joyful in hope, patient** in affliction, *faithful* in prayer. Share with the Lord's people who are in need. *Practice hospitality.*
>
> *Bless* those who persecute you; *bless* and do not *curse*. **Rejoice** with those who rejoice; **mourn** with those who mourn. *Live in harmony* with one another. Do not be **proud**, but be *willing to associate* with people of low position. Do not be *conceited*. (Rom. 12:9–16)

We should not overlook a final set of corporate emotions that Christians are exhorted to cultivate—rejoicing, singing, and giving thanks. Repeatedly Christians are told to rejoice, to be thankful and to express this, and to engage in singing (Pss. 9:11; 149:1; Eph. 5:18–21; Col. 3:16). This is an especially important instruction to consider as part of the Christian whole-life philosophy.

Here's the question: Why would Christians be instructed to sing songs of praise and to consciously express thanksgiving to God, even in the midst of trials, difficulties, and uncertainties? The answer: Because the Christian philosophy understands the complex relationship between our minds, bodies, actions, and emotions. In line with the thoughtful Aristotelian tradition on emotions, the Old and New Testaments teach people to act in certain ways, knowing that cognitive and volitional choices not only *reflect* our emotions but also *affect and educate* them. As we engage in certain practices, both individually and corporately, they shape and form us. The liturgies and habits of the church educate our emotions in certain ways, giving articulation to and expression of certain emotional states, carrying us along with them even while our emotions may be more or less disordered and inadequately trained. We are commended to do things that include and are motivated by particular emotions, because there is a place for duty on the way to virtue. We educate our emotions through action, eventually finding the wholeness of body and soul.

○ ○ ○ ○

In London in 2014 a group of more than three hundred people interested in Stoicism as a philosophy of life gathered together for the first "Stoicon." As the organizers noted, this was probably the largest gathering of Stoics in over two thousand years, if not ever! The conference has continued in various cities ever since, including the special location of Athens for Stoicon 2019. Stoicon is organized by the nonprofit group Modern Stoicism, one of a number of groups and websites, such as DailyStoic .com, that are promoting the rediscovery of Stoicism to help people live in the modern world. As Daily Stoic describes it, this is a philosophy "for those of us who live our lives in the real world"—not high-brow speculative stuff.[10]

An internet search of "Stoicism" will result in not just translations of classic Stoic works by Epictetus, Seneca, and Marcus Aurelius but also a slate of modern books promoting the rediscovery and application of Stoicism for today's readers. These books, sites, newsletters, and conferences offer practical advice on mastering one's emotions, learning to meditate morning and night, and practicing certain virtues. You can even buy attractive brass coins that contain artistic images and Latin sayings like *memento mori* (remember your own mortality) and *premeditatio malorum* (premeditation on evils/misfortunes) that remind owners of key Stoic ideas (see fig. 12).

Figure 12. Stoicism coins, used by modern practitioners to remind them of core Stoic practices such as *amor fati* and *premeditatio malorum*

Modern life is filled with stresses, anxieties, disappointments, frustrations in relationships and work, and fears about the future. Health scares, worries about the safety of our children, pain in marriage, job loss—all of these situations evoke many emotions that can be overwhelming. Stoicism's practical habits of focusing our energy only on what we can control—our choices and our emotional responses—are very helpful. I'll go out on a limb and say that I think Stoicism is probably the second-best philosophy available to humans because of its emphasis on being centered, emotionally stable, and developing constructive virtues. If I weren't a Christian, I would buy the coins, practice the morning and night meditations, read books like Donald Robertson's *How to Think like a Roman Emperor* and Ryan Holiday's *The Obstacle Is the Way*, and seek to live by educating my emotions through Stoic practices.

I still do a lot of those things. But I believe there is a philosophy of the emotional life that is more comprehensive and effective than even the best of Stoicism—the Christian philosophy. And beyond practicality, the Christian philosophy also has the distinct advantage of being true—rooted in the historical and theological reality of the incarnation, life, death, resurrection, and ascension of Jesus. It is a philosophy for the whole of life rooted in a metaphysic more comprehensive than Stoicism.

The Christian philosophy is indeed "for those of us who live our lives in the real world." It is a religious philosophy that includes divine revelation and revealed ethics. Christianity has nuanced, complicated, and lofty theological constructs. But for all that, it is no less practical when it comes to our complex emotional lives. Indeed, because of its height, depth, and complexity, the whole-life Christian philosophy provides a robust and far-reaching practical approach to our emotions.

○ ○ ○ ○

So let's drill down into the practicality of the Christian philosophy of emotions. We can summarize Christianity's practical advice on emotions with two habits to develop and practice. If I were to make two "Christoicism" coins for sale, they would have these two words on them—"Reflection" and "Prayer."

Reflection. As in Stoicism and all good philosophies and therapies, the Christian philosophy holds that our minds need to be intentionally engaged for growth, healing, and happiness to occur. To philosophize is to learn to love wisdom. This occurs in the circular dialogue between thinking and practice, between learning and trying. Key to all of this is the habit of *intentional reflection.*

We can take an appreciative look at the Stoics' playbook. The Stoics taught and practiced that essential to living a balanced and happy life was the practice of reflecting on what is true. Each morning a good Stoic will think about what they might face that day and role-play how they could approach a situation so as to not get hooked emotionally. Comparably, at night a Stoic will conclude each day by reflecting on ways he or she could have been more virtuous and could have been more reflective and wise. All of this is soaked through with regular meditation on the fragility of one's own life and even intentional meditation on misfortunes to fortify resolve to live each day fully (*premeditatio malorum*). Many such practices are utilized today not just by adherents of modern Stoicism but also by therapists and life coaches. And they generally help people.

The good in this kind of intentional reflection is that, as Socrates famously said, "The unexamined life is not worth living." This is because without intentional reflection, we will live our lives without direction and purpose. Or worse, we will live with misdirected and distorted goals. Reflection and meditation are essential to living well because they educate our emotions in robust and healthy ways, providing the nutrients to our soul's emotional soil.

When we turn to the Bible, we see that Christianity encourages a comparable but superiorly shaped version of such reflective practices. Examples of intentional reflection abound. Immediately after the great Shema is given (Deut. 6:4–5), God's people are instructed to regularly reflect on these truths, remember them, and teach them to the next generation verbally and with symbolic reminders: "Impress them on your children. Talk about them when you sit at home and when you walk along the road, when you lie down and when you get up. Tie them as symbols on your hands and bind them on your foreheads. Write them on the doorframes of your houses and on your gates" (6:7–9).

This habit of intentional reflection has a shaping effect on the belief, faithfulness, obedience, and thereby emotional health of the Israelites. The book of Psalms, which is the epicenter of the Bible's emotional education, begins with a remarkably similar vision. Psalm 1 starts with a vivid image of what kind of people are truly happy and flourishing (a fruit-bearing tree planted by streams of water, 1:3) versus those whose lives end up in regret and loss and destruction (chaff in the wind, 1:4).

One is clearly the Good Life and the other is not. What is the difference? The happy are those who meditate or intentionally reflect on God's ways and instructions day and night, a delightful endeavor (1:2). The opposite of this kind of life of reflection is the life of being carried along with the activities of the wicked (1:1). Intentional reflection directed toward God is the difference.

Psalm 1 directly feeds into Jesus's own teachings on true happiness in the Beatitudes (Matt. 5:3–12). With variations on the same tune, Jesus defines true happiness as found in certain ways of seeing and being in the world centered on his revelation of the kingdom of heaven. Once again, this happiness and subsequent life of discipleship depends on learning to reflect on the true nature of reality as taught by Jesus. Our emotions and our behaviors are educated by particular reflections.

The whole of the Sermon on the Mount invites us into seeing and being in the world through reflection. But even more specifically, Jesus addresses particular emotions and provides a pedagogy of our emotions through God-directed meditation. In Matthew 6:25–34 Jesus focuses our attention on one of the most powerful and destructive human emotions: anxiety. He knows the natural human propensity to worry, and he addresses the most fundamental human anxiety—the daily sustenance of food, water, and clothing. These are but examples of all of the anxieties we face in daily life. Jesus says plainly and triply, "Do not worry" (6:25, 31, 34). On what basis, Jesus? Is the solution to anxiety found in the advice of Bobby McFerrin's affected reggae-style song "Don't Worry, Be Happy"? Is that Jesus's method?

No, Jesus's practical advice for dealing with anxiety is not a denial of the reality of problems (Buddhism's solution), nor detachment from the uncontrollable world (Stoicism), nor blithe whistleable songs (McFerrin), but intentional reflection on what is true. Particularly, the focus of this directed reflection is on

125

the Father God, who is willing and able to provide for his children's needs. The heavenly Father knows that we need certain things, and there is ample evidence of his care and provision in the world of flowers and birds around us. The practice of intentionally reflecting on these truths does not magically make all anxieties disappear, nor does it deny the ongoing reality of negative emotions in our human, limited lives. But it does provide a practical means by which we can educate our emotions.

Other examples abound in both the Old and New Testaments, such as Philippians 4:8, which sums up succinctly the way of being Christian in the world: "Finally, brothers and sisters, whatever is true, whatever is noble, whatever is right, whatever is pure, whatever is lovely, whatever is admirable—if anything is excellent or praiseworthy—*think about such things.*"

○○○○

Prayer—Confession and Supplication. The discussion of how Jesus instructs us regarding anxiety leads naturally into the second practice of emotional education in the Christian philosophy—prayer, both confession (seeking forgiveness) and supplication (making requests). Herein lies a crucial difference between the Christian philosophy and all others—the fundamental belief that there is a God who is personal, relatable, capable, and kind. This God, first revealed to the patriarchs and then finally manifested through Jesus, invites people into a covenantal relationship of love. Prayer in the form of both confession and supplication is central to this relationship.

By way of contrast, for Stoicism, Buddhism, or any of a variety of other philosophies that offer practical guidance on how to live well, ultimately one's own self-sufficiency is the core and foundation. This is why the massive genre of books in this area is called *self*-help. Books of this genre at the airport or your local used bookshop all say the same thing: ultimately, it is up to you to find happiness, health, and peace. For the Stoics, this is most explicit: self-sufficiency is the goal—dependence on no one and no circumstance is required for your happiness. The only way to find *ataraxia* and *eudaimonia* is to limit your emotional responses and learn to focus only on your own virtue, not circumstances that are out of your control.

There is a lot of truth in this advice, and indeed countless people have been helped by some version of this counsel. I often tell my children the same. When they are agitated with someone else or worried about some potential problem, I often remind them that they can't control anyone else's actions or responses, but they can and should pay attention to their own choices and emotional health.

But the Christian philosophy offers so much more, rooted in its theological metaphysic of belief in a personal and capable God. Prayer in the form of confession and supplication adds the active ingredient into a life of emotional vibrancy and health. Through confessional prayer, Christianity is able to deal with some of our most devastating emotions—shame and guilt. These powerful and destructive emotions are an inevitable part of the human experience. But other philosophies have no clear way to deal with the devastating power of these emotions other than denying that they are real or trying to talk oneself into a place of acceptance of our limits and responsibilities, or both.

Christianity acknowledges that guilt and shame are real emotions and are based on moral realities—that there is a Good coming from the true God and that it can be violated, resulting in both guilt and shame. And then Christianity provides a powerful means by which to face the reality of these damaging emotions and receive release from them, not through denial or self-help talk, but through repentance and forgiveness. Other philosophies' approach to guilt and shame is akin to turning up the radio and putting electrical tape over the check engine light when your van is making horrible noises. Christianity handles guilt and shame the way a surgeon handles a cancerous tumor—by cutting in and cutting out to provide full healing. This happens through prayers of confession.

When King David seduced Bathsheba and then had her husband Uriah killed, this once joyful and wholehearted man of God found himself depressed, numb, and drained of emotional and physical energy. He was burdened with guilt and shame that he could not face in himself, though its effects were felt: "When I kept silent, my bones wasted away through my groaning all day long. For day and night your hand was heavy on me; my strength was sapped as in the heat of summer" (Ps. 32:3–4).

When he was finally confronted by the prophet Nathan, David broke down and confessed his sin (2 Sam. 12:1–13). The result was emotional release, healing, and restoration of balance and psychological health. He describes the forgiveness he receives as happiness/flourishing and the cause for rejoicing: "Happy is the one whose transgressions are forgiven, whose sins are covered. Happy is the one whose sin the LORD does not count against them and in whose spirit is no deceit. . . . Rejoice in the LORD and be glad, you righteous; sing, all you who are upright in heart!" (Ps. 32:1–2, 11, my translation).

Another form of prayer—supplication—also plays an important part in Christianity's philosophy of emotions. Once again we can helpfully compare the Bible's vision to that of Stoicism. The genius of Stoicism is that it is indeed very freeing to let go of the expectation that circumstances will provide our happiness. Happiness is found in managing our emotional responses, not the circumstances themselves, Stoicism says. As we have noted earlier, there is a disagreement here between the Stoics and their predecessors in the Aristotelian tradition. Aristotle argued that our circumstances, our Fortune, are a factor in our happiness. Emotions can and should be educated, but there is a reality to the fact that some people have better lives than others, and this does inevitably affect happiness.

In this, Christianity aligns more closely with the Aristotelian tradition than the purely Stoic, yet once again with an important nuance. It is true, according to the Bible, that our experiences and our circumstances have an effect on our happiness. God cares about our happiness and continually promises provision and a space and time when the world will be set right, when death, destruction, pain, and tears will be removed. This is envisioned in the Old Testament, with a shadow of its reality at the height of King David's and King Solomon's reigns. But things fall apart, always. And in the case of Israel, completely. The prophets increasingly look forward to a time when God would restore the world. This is Christianity's understanding—that this restoration of God's complete and perfect reign upon the earth has been inaugurated and guaranteed through Jesus's life, death, and resurrection. This is what all the "kingdom of God" talk in the New Testament is about. There is a time and place of perfect circumstances coming, resulting in perfect shalom for God's people. Our future is not to reach a state of enlightenment that supersedes our circumstances—disconnected from reality—but for God to bring peace and flourishing to the real world.

Christianity is a forward-looking faith that sees ultimate human happiness as something that will occur fully in the future, because God himself will vanquish all evil and be fully present with his creation. So circumstances do matter. Denial and escapism are not the solution. At the center of the greatest Christian prayer, the Lord's Prayer, is the supplication for God to come and set the world to right, for the heavenly reality to become the earthly reality:

> Our Father who is in heaven,
>> Let your name be sanctified,

Let your kingdom come,
Let your will be done,
As these are in heaven, let them be also on earth.
(Matt. 6:9–10, my translation)[11]

And yet at the same time, Christians can and should learn to rejoice, to know joy and peace and flourishing, even when circumstances are *not* conducive. How? Through prayers of supplication, offering ourselves to God and asking him to provide and care for us. Through prayerfully entrusting our lives and circumstances and emotions to a personal God who is both compassionate and capable, Christians can find emotional health. A great example of this is found in Peter's words to anxious Christians: "Cast all your anxiety on him because he cares for you" (1 Pet. 5:7). God cares. And he is also capable. God's "mighty hand" will lift his people up in due time (5:6). Christians can do more than just tell themselves that everything will be fine. Christians can do more than just tell themselves that circumstances don't matter. Real situations affect us. The great Christian hope is that we can supplicate. We can ask a compassionate, personal, and capable God to intervene, help, provide, and deliver.

RESTORING
RELATIONSHIPS

The Necessity of Relationships

Pulitzer Prize–winning author Wallace Stegner's last novel was a beautiful, semiautobiographical story entitled *Crossing to Safety*.[1] The reader experiences three and a half decades of the relationship between two couples, the Langs and the Morgans. The story is poignant in its stern realism, engulfing readers with, as one publisher fairly describes it, "quiet majesty, deep compassion, and powerful insight."[2] *Crossing to Safety* is a long and winding story not about great events or illicit affairs and their tawdry details but about friendship, about learning to find true "safety" through relationship with others.

The narrator, Larry Morgan, reflects on the complexities, joys, and frustrations of this foursome's lives together as one of them lies dying. We hear Larry's profound musings on the great gift of friendship. He observes that friendship is "a relationship that has no formal shape, there are no rules or obligations or bonds as in marriage or the family, it is held together by neither law nor property nor blood, there is no glue in it but mutual liking. It is therefore rare."[3]

The rarity of this kind of friendship is tragic because it is loving relationships that give shape, direction, and fulfillment to our lives. Reflecting on Stegner's presentation of friendship,

Terry Tempest Williams describes it this way: It is "love and friendship, the sanctity and celebration of our relationships, that not only support a good life, but create one."[4]

In other words, relationships aren't an add-on to life, they *make up* our life.

Stegner is not alone is his assessment. In an issue published just a couple years after his death, the *Bulletin of the American Psychological Association* contained an article entitled "The Need to Belong: Desire for Interpersonal Attachments as a Fundamental Human Motivation."[5] In language infinitely less lucid and enjoyable than Stegner's, researchers Roy Baumeister and Mark Leary report that for humans to experience satisfaction and flourishing they must have "frequent, affectively pleasant interactions with a few other people" and that "these interactions must take place in the context of a temporally stable and enduring framework of affective concern for each other's welfare."[6] In nonacademic verbiage: we need friendships.

Baumeister and Leary's "belonging hypothesis" suggests that the central driving psychological factor for humans is not, as Freud suggested, learned sexuality and aggression but rather the innate (and therefore universal) need to form and maintain interpersonal relationships. These psychologists review many studies about attachments people make (or fail to make) and the effect of these on mental health. They note studies that have shown that in certain situations even bitter rivals and prejudiced people can come to work together (for example, the Robbers Cave study), showing the natural need and desire to bond with other people.

These reflections on friendship, whether in powerful narrative form or academic jargon, are articulating something we all know—relationships are necessary to our flourishing. Relationships in the home, in towns and communities, and in religious and other affiliations form the framework and fabric of society itself. A lack of relationship with others breeds distortion, dark-ness, and often destruction to oneself or others.

○ ○ ○ ○

As we found in our discussion of emotions, what today's psy-chologists and therapists describe and prescribe for relationships was in ancient times explored and explicated by the philoso-phers. The importance of relationships of all kinds—marital, familial, friendly, societal, occupational, governmental—was a central theme in the ancient philosophers' teaching and prac-tice, on par with the grand topic of emotions. Different phi-losophers offered varying ideas on what friendship is, what marriages should look like, how children should be treated, and how people should relate to each other in society. But they all understood that to find and promote human flourishing, the Good Life, we must attend to these issues and develop inten-tional habits in all of our relationships.

As with our discussion of emotions, our understanding of Christianity as a whole-life philosophy is best discerned and articulated by examining the "cultural encyclopedia" that surrounds, intersects with, and influences it—this means the context of ancient philosophy. Christianity does not exist in an isolated cultural and conceptual vacuum. Quite the contrary, Christianity is happily seeking to understand, speak into, and transform real people living in real cultures. This necessarily includes our relationships.

And frankly, even apart from providing a context for under-standing Christianity, there is simply a lot of wisdom to be found in the ancient philosophers' reflections on relationships. These were great thinkers who pondered well what kind of structures and personal relationships best benefit society and promote flourishing. No ancient philosopher worth his salt could offer any kind of philosophy of life without addressing the complex series of human relationships, from marriage to societal structures. And so they did. And thoughtful Christians have long "plundered the Egyptians" to gather gems from the storehouses of human wisdom and reflection. So too should we.

○ ○ ○ ○

Being the best man at a modern wedding, if done well, entails a lot of responsibility, not the least of which is the best man's speech. Such a speech can be either the source of a long-winded, awkward, and poorly executed several minutes of cringe, or, less frequently, a funny and engaging, meaningful tribute to the new couple. Most of the time it is somewhere in between.

The origins of this speech are somewhat murky, but the idea of sage advice delivered to newlyweds is as old as the hills. The philosopher Plutarch (AD 46–120), in a well-meaning avuncular way, wrote a pithy forty-eight-part essay, "Advice to Bride and Groom," that became very famous and is still read today.

The bride and groom Plutarch addresses were named Eurydice and Pollianus, and they may have been relatives of his, though obviously the advice applies to any who have ears to hear. As Plutarch says in his introductory remarks, "Of the many admirable themes contained in philosophy, that which deals with marriage deserves no less serious attention than any other, for by means of it philosophy weaves a spell over those who are entering together into a lifelong partnership, and renders them gentle and amiable toward each other."[7] We might translate the "weaves a spell" today with a less magical-sounding phrase such as "binds together," but the point is the same: married couples need sound philosophical advice if they are to have a happy marriage.

With two thousand years of cultural and chronological distance, Plutarch's advice is at once familiar and odd. He advises the young couple that physical beauty and passion won't last

Figure 13. Plutarch

Delphi Archaeological Museum, CC BY-SA / Wikimedia Commons

forever, so they should build their relationship on character and wisdom (sec. 4). Husbands and wives should not talk about things being "mine" or "not mine" but, following Plato, treat everything that matters to them as common property (sec. 20). They should try to avoid fighting with each other, but especially in the bedchamber, because this should be a place of mutual love and connection (sec. 39). All sounds good.

From the "odd-to-us" category, we are advised that the wife should nibble a quince (look it up) before bed (sec. 1), and that she should not use love potions and magic spells to try to control her husband but instead use virtue (sec. 5). Also, she should not be upset when her husband gets drunk and has a little peccadillo with one of the maidservants; this is done out of respect—when he is feeling wild, he doesn't bring her into such revelries (sec. 16).

Above all—and this is in the concluding and longest section of Plutarch's "Advice"—a woman should be fully educated in philosophy, just like her husband. This is so that she can learn wisdom, not be deceived by foolish ideas, and share in her husband's intellectual advancement for their mutual flourishing (sec. 48). Philosophy matters in marriage.

Plutarch is not alone in giving marriage advice, even if his feels more personal. As a Greek philosopher living in the Roman era, he represents a long tradition of philosophical discussion of the marital relationship. In *The Republic*, Plato's monumental treatise on how to structure society, we find sentiments that are even more unsettling than Plutarch's—namely, that wives and children be held in common and breeding be eugenically controlled by the city-state guardians through arranged temporary marriages, with the state then raising the children for the good of all. Plato's point was to extend what are natural family sympathies to the whole state.

Aristotle's own take, in his equally important *Politics*, differs sharply. Natural familial love can't and won't be transferred to everyone, Aristotle argues. The city-state is not one big communal mass but the built-up compilation of smaller units, with individual male and female procreative units (stable marriages) as the foundation. Throughout the ancient philosophical understanding, marriage primarily functioned in economic, political, and social ways. Marriage in its best forms might include a harmonious affection, but its primary shape was social, to create bonds across families, to control inheritance, and to share resources and labor.[8]

In the Roman Empire, the philosophical reflection on the importance of marriage continues and is adjusted. Building on

Aristotle's vision, the Roman Empire family unit was part of the layered cosmos. The emperor himself was portrayed as the head of the household-empire, and Julius Caesar took on the title *pater patriae*, "father of the fathers." The household was to be ordered well, because this reflected and ordered the whole empire.

Thus, the philosophers often wrote "household codes" that gave specific instructions for the various members in the family unit—husbands, wives, children, slaves, and servants. This order, which was eventually codified in various marriage laws, was understood as a microcosm of the whole empire's structure. The household was "the seed-bed of the state" (Cicero).[9] Marriage and households are that important for the Good Life.

○ ○ ○ ○

I don't live in the *state* of Kentucky; I live in the *commonwealth* of Kentucky. On paper, the fifty United States of America actually consists of forty-six states and four commonwealths—in addition to Kentucky, the other nonstate states are Massachusetts, Pennsylvania, and Virginia. In reality, the word "commonwealth" in the legal constitutions of these four bordered entities means nothing practically; they have the same kinds of laws, elections, and relationship to the federal government as the "regular" states. But for many political thinkers at the time of the founding of these four early governments, people like framer John Adams, the term "commonwealth" was better than "state" because it communicated more clearly an antimonarchical sentiment.[10] "Republic," "state," "commonwealth," and "democracy" are all terms and concepts that were foundational to the creation and shape of the colonial revolution that became the United States of America.

The government of these "United States" has a flag that citizens are regularly invited to pledge themselves to as representative of "the Republic for which it stands, one nation, under

God, indivisible, with liberty and justice for all." These words and sentiments sound so familiar to most modern readers (at least the Americans) that we may not realize their significance. Each of these words has an important history that consciously goes back far beyond the founding of the United States into the philosophical discussion of ancient Greece and Rome. It is no mere coincidence that Monticello—President Thomas Jefferson's home, which is pictured on the US nickel—looks like it was transplanted from Athens and that a copy of Seneca was on Jefferson's nightstand when he died. The French and American revolutions were a kind of reappropriation of ancient Greek thought on societal relationships. The ancient philosophers realized that their philosophies needed to explore important questions about politics and government. The revolutionaries of the eighteenth century realized the same.

So what are the great questions of politics and government? They include explorations like Who gets to decide laws? and How do we enforce them? And more deeply, What is the role of government? What is a just government? What obligations does it have toward the people it governs, and vice versa? But above all of these questions, really the two interrelated questions of political philosophy are these: What is the Good Life? and, How do you structure society to promote the Good Life?

Every political system and stump speech has underneath it—sometimes unconsciously—its own answers to these foundational questions, whether it's Trump's "Make America Great Again," Obama's "Yes We Can," Hoover's "A Chicken in Every Pot and a Car in Every Garage," or Lincoln's "Union, Liberty, Peace." Politics are built on a vision for what the Good is and how to achieve it.

As we have seen in other aspects of philosophy, each thinker's political philosophy is the practical application of his or her metaphysics—different philosophical systems' understanding of what the world is and what is good. Author Anne Rooney observes that political philosophy is rooted in metaphysics because it requires defining "concepts such as justice, freedom, authority and fairness and then finding social structures in which they can be implemented."[11] This is no small matter.

So why talk about political philosophy under the category of relationships? It is because *politeia*, the constitutional and visionary structure of society, is a matter of relationships between people. Politics are simply relationships writ large and codified into structures that are required once a collection of human relationships expands beyond a basic family unit. This was explicitly the concept of marriage and empire in the Roman era, as we saw above. How to structure such relationships for the Good is rightly the purview of the philosophers.

○ ○ ○ ○

The idea that politics is a kind of relationship between individuals and society is called a "social contract" and first appears in Plato. The philosophers, recall, sought to build a society based on intentional thought about the nature of reality (metaphysics) and the Good (ethics). This was self-consciously very different from the mythological polytheistic approach of an earlier Greek era or the Persian and other ancient Near Eastern views that emphasized the divine appointment of emperors and governments. Rather, as Plato describes it in *The Republic*, society should be structured in ways that reflect the good of the Ideal Forms. He envisioned an ideal society where citizens know how to best use their talents to benefit society and do so with virtue, for the good of everyone. The focus for Plato is on structuring society and government for the republic's flourishing, by which everyone would then benefit and experience the Good. This ideal and hierarchically stratified society, according to Plato, would be led by an elite class of guardians who were trained in

141

philosophy and the arts of war and government to lead well.[12] The king was a philosopher. The city was the goal.

While Plato's *Republic* was a massive achievement in thought, it was not without its critics. Plato's most famous pupil, Aristotle, had a decidedly different opinion. Aristotle agreed that society needed to be intentionally structured and led according to philosophical principles—the Good pursued by virtuous people, with flourishing as the goal. But beyond that, he offered a very different view of politics that reflected his own experience at the highest level of government in Greece as well as his travels throughout the broader empire.

Aristotle's political philosophy comes to us in his book entitled *Politics*. The English word "political" comes from the Greek *politikos*, meaning "pertaining to the *polis* [city-state]." (We also have cities that have combined other titles with this Greek word, such as Minneapolis, Indianapolis, and Annapolis.) The *polis* or city-state was how Greek society was structured in his day. And it's all about relationships.

For Aristotle, the study of political philosophy was a subset of one of the three big categories of his understanding of the world: contemplative (physics and metaphysics), practical (ethics), and productive (how to make useful and beautiful objects). Politics fits under practical understanding, which has as its goal prescriptions for how to live according to the Good, or as we would call it today, ethics. In fact, Aristotle's *Politics* refers often to its companion work, the *Nicomachean Ethics*. As the *Stanford Encyclopedia of Philosophy* describes it, "Politics is a practical science, since it is concerned with the noble action or happiness of the citizens. . . . [It is] a normative or prescriptive discipline rather than a purely empirical or descriptive inquiry."[13]

So what does Aristotle prescribe? With the aim of the happiness of its citizens, the city-state should be governed by a constitution (a *politeia*) that is like the soul is to any living organism; the constitution defines and guides the aims of the society. (Sound familiar to Americans?) In classic Aristotelian analytical style, he examines different types of societal structures, evaluating each for their strengths and weaknesses and their possible deviant forms. Aristotle argues that the end goal of enabling virtuous citizens to flourish must be the evaluative tool for determining which form of government is best.

Therefore, society should not be structured as a business enterprise designed to maximize wealth (as an oligarchy would have it), nor should government exist to promote equality for everyone (as the democracy proponents would argue). Such a utopian scheme of shared power was unrealistic and went against the principle of justice and merit. Rather, the city-state is a community (*koinōnia*)—a collection of various relationships (households, economic classes, political units) that have shared interests, hence their communal unity. Ultimately, these parts are made up of individual citizens who learn their shared way of life from the constitution or organizing principles (*politeia*).[14] Again, it's all about relationships.

The city-state should focus on the Good and what promotes living accordingly. In this, Aristotle was critical of Plato for focusing too much on the city-state's form rather than its goal—which is the flourishing of virtuous individuals. Also unlike Plato's idealistic vision in *The Republic*, Aristotle's *Politics* was practical, recognizing that humans are imperfect and compromises need to be made. Practically, the *polis* should be ruled by a group of middle-class people, not a tyrant, not the rich, and not the poor, all of whom would have interests in conflict with the flourishing of the virtuous.[15]

To keep all this organized there must be a sovereign ruler, a lawgiver who is virtuous himself, a craftsman who shapes the *polis* for its good.[16] In fact, the model or example of the virtuous monarch is more important than the writing of specific laws. Laws are flawed and can never fully reflect the ideal social ethos; this is why the constitution (*politeia*) is more than its written form but is a vision and way of life. Really, the best constitution is a good person, an exemplar of virtue whose life functions as a "living law." Such a person is rightly the king. It may not be realistic for the king himself to be a philosopher, but he should be educated in and advised by philosophy, because it alone enables flourishing. (I hope you're already thinking ahead to how Jesus will be presented as a Philosopher-King.)

Over time these ideas develop and change. We could talk about how the Good of the *polis* shifts more toward the flourishing of the individual with the Stoics and Epicureans. But the important point is this—the Good Life depends on structuring society with good relationships, which is why this is such an important topic in philosophy.

○ ○ ○ ○

Throughout the 1980s the Hasbro toy company struck plastic gold with a series of colorful toy horses. Over 150 million My Little Ponies (MLP) were sold in that decade. In what is often derided as manipulative commercialization of children, in 1986 and 1987 Sunbow and Marvel Productions created an animated television series to accompany and boost the sales of the toys. I was too old to be a fan of MLP at the time, but I remember well how ubiquitous the show and the plastic ponies were.

After various horsey iterations over the following years, in 2010 Hasbro again found success with another version of this equestrian fantasy world (and merchandise): *My Little Pony: Friendship Is Magic* (MLP:FIM). Running from 2010 to 2019 (with some ongoing spin-offs) this version is markedly different and more complex than the previous show. As the creator of the new series remarked, the 1980s show was quite shallow and depicted the ponies having "endless tea parties" where the girl ponies "giggled over nothing and defeated villains by either sharing with them or crying."[17] By intentional contrast, the *MLP:FIM* series is surprisingly sophisticated, with in-depth characters, engaging story lines, and catchy music—all with an ironic and postmodern allusive intertextual feel.

I say all this as one who watched the series quite reluctantly at first, sitting next to my youngest daughter on the couch. I became a fan (along with countless other more-committed-than-me male believers, called bronies). Like with any good children's story, adults realize there is more going on in *MLP:FIM* than what appears on the surface.

Baked into the plot of the show is the theme of friendship, as the subtitle indicates. However, it's not a trite and shallow treatment of friendship, as the animated genre may incline one to think. Rather, it is startlingly profound. The main characters (Twilight, Applejack, Rarity, Fluttershy, Rainbow Dash, and Pinkie Pie), each with their own nonstereotypical personalities, represent different aspects of friendship. Over the long narrative arc of the show, they learn that being friends involves conflict, forgiveness, and difference but that the longed-for "Harmony" (translate: shalom, human flourishing) can only be found through such real and complicated relationships.

I realize I've taken a risk here in confessing my appreciation for an animated show targeted for preadolescent girls. But the skepticism that non-*MLP:FIM*-believers have about how magical ponies could contribute to our understanding of friendship is revealing of a bigger cultural change. In recent centuries, the idea of wholehearted and affectionate friendship is something that is often relegated to children and their cartoons. As Tolkien observed, the same thing disastrously happened with fantasy literature in the late nineteenth century—it got removed from acceptance as an adult genre and relegated to the nursery, like old furniture that keeps getting moved to less visible places in the house.[18] But this shift creates a loss for both adults and children.

So too with the topic of friendship. We lose something when we think of friendship as something especially important for children. Close, intimate, affectionate friendship between adults of the same gender was a central theme in ancient philosophical discourse. And more importantly, it was part of people's everyday lives. Friendship—what it is, what different forms it takes, why it is important, and how to develop it—was one of the largest and most important topics in philosophy, precisely because it was such an important experience at all levels of society.

Accordingly, I've saved this discussion of friendship for the last and most prominent place in our exploration of what ancient writers had to say about various relationships.

○ ○ ○ ○

Some subgroups of people unfairly get a bad rap because their views and practices are out of sync with their culture. Groups of people who are committed to certain ideals and who endeavor to live that way are often derided by the majority culture because they provide some kind of psychological threat or challenge to the way most people live. As a result, such an idealistic subgroup is often caricatured, with their views twisted and misrepresented to such an extent that their name becomes a byline for all that is bad.

This was the case with the Epicureans, a group of people committed to living according to the principles of their inspiring leader and exemplar, Epicurus (341–270 BC). Though Epicurus is now considered one of the most important Hellenistic philosophers, in his own day and for many subsequent centuries, Epicureanism was written off as mere hedonism. Some said the followers of Epicurus, who lived together at his house-school in Athens called the Garden, were engaged in sexual orgies and living for mere shallow pleasures. It was derided as hedonism, not philosophy.

Nothing could be further from the truth. Epicurus was not opposed to pleasure, certainly, but his views were very nuanced. And nuanced ideas are easily misrepresented. The Epicureans were intentionally pursuing the greatest pleasure—*ataraxia* (tranquility and peace) and *aponia* (the absence of pain). But these can only be attained, according to their teacher, by banishing the fear of death and suffering and instead living present to daily life, including its pleasures of food and relationships (in moderation). The Epicureans were just countercultural enough to be written off as deranged—but unfairly.

Central to the Epicurean philosophical pursuit of the full pleasure of life was friendship. The Epicureans' cultural crime? They dared to live as *friends*. Men and women dwelt together at the Garden, discussing a wide range of philosophical topics, reflecting on metaphysics, epistemology, ethics, and society. The other Athenian philosophical schools such as the Stoa and Aristotle's Academy also made disciples and taught comprehensive philosophical views, but no one rivaled the Epicureans for their commitment to the pursuit of a communal way of life rooted in friendship.

Epicurus taught that all humans desire the peace and happiness/blessedness (*makarios*) that the gods alone have. The most efficacious way to attain that goal is through friendship. "Friendship," Epicurus said, "dances around the world, calling on us all to awaken to happiness."[19] Our maximum felicity in life comes through the kind of security, pleasure, and wisdom that committed friendships alone can provide. Of all the things that wisdom provides to people to live a fully happy life, Epicurus observed, the greatest "by far is the possession of friendship."[20]

○ ○ ○ ○

Even though the Epicureans attracted detractors for being out of sync with the rest of the philosophical schools, all the philosophers agreed about the importance of friendship. Even before this subject became central in philosophy, friendship was often extoled through the great myths and stories of the ancient world. Many examples of noble and affectionate friends can be found in the cultural narratives of ancient Greece and Rome—warrior friends like Achilles and Patroclus in the *Iliad* and Theseus and Pirithous in the poetry of Ovid. The philosophers promoted these sentiments, adding deep reflections on the nature and pursuit of friendship.

The fountainhead of much of the discussion of friendship for the last twenty-three hundred years is Aristotle. In the *Nichomachean Ethics*, his book of wisdom written for his son, two of the ten sections, about one-fifth of the whole book, are dedicated to an exploration of friendship. In classic Aristotelian no-stone-left-unturned analysis, he explores many facets of what makes up friendship, including nuances that go beyond what we need to discuss here but are definitely worth reading.

Aristotle's threefold classification of types of friendship (*philia*) is recognized as his most influential contribution:[21]

- Friendships of utility—relationships based on need or help given to another
- Friendships of pleasure—mutual enjoyment of each other with shared values and interests
- Friendships of virtue—love and concern for the other's welfare, focusing on what one can give more than receive

It is this third form of friendship that is the most excellent, the most enduring, and the most rare, requiring two people who are truly virtuous. In this ideal kind of friendship alone we can find in a friend "another self." A virtuous person is one with himself or herself (harmonious; whole), and when they find another virtuous person, they find another soul with whom to live life well. In this way, virtuous friendship is the bridge that links the virtuous individual to other people, groups, and society.[22]

Aristotle was not the only thinker to philosophize about friendship. Plato did so before him and others would after. In general, in the Hellenistic era friendship was understood as a matter of loyalty, mutual support, and equality. Diogenes summed up Aristotle's view of friendship as "an equality of reciprocal good-will."[23] Or in the phrase of my seventy-two-year-old friend Bob, friendship is "a sweet obligation." These Greek philosophers bequeath to history sophisticated views on the goodness and beauty of the highest form of human relationships: friendship.

○ ○ ○ ○

In the Roman philosophical tradition, the name Cicero is well known because of his important role in society (he was a consul and augur) and the many influential writings he left behind. This includes his treatise on friendship, *De amicitia*, whose title we can translate as *How to Be a Friend*.[24] But referring to this author only as Cicero reflects what often happens with famous people from a faraway land and time. We forget that he was a real person—Marcus Tullius Cicero—who knew the grief of losing a daughter and who experienced the heady heights of being a power player in the Roman Empire only to lose this and taste the anxiety and pain of being old and exiled far from his former home. And he knew friendship.

Marcus's closest friend was Titus Pomponius, who went by the name Atticus. These devoted friends wrote affectionate letters to each other over the course of the decades of the first century BC. Cicero's *How to Be a Friend* was dedicated to Atticus, and it has become one of the most well-known and arguably best treatments of what friendship is. As scholar and translator Philip Freeman notes, Cicero was influenced by the earlier Greek writings, but he "goes beyond his predecessors and creates in this short work a compelling guide to finding, keeping and appreciating those people in our lives we value not for what they can give us, but because we find in them a kindred soul."[25] Cicero's piece is inspiring and practical, exhorting virtuous people to treat others according to the Golden Rule, to avoid flattery, to intentionally cultivate new friendships while maintaining the old ones as well, and to seek friends, remembering that life is joyless without them.

○ ○ ○ ○

Building on this strong ancient foundation, friendship remained a focal point in philosophical discussion and real-life experience well into the nineteenth century. There are many accounts of famous and unexpected friendships between people as diverse as Mark Twain and Helen Keller, Hunter Thompson and Pat Buchanan, and T. S. Eliot and Groucho Marx. We know about these largely through the now-lost habit of long letter writing between friends. Such correspondence often provides later biographers with evidence of the great affection and dedication such relationships had. They also show how self-consciously aware people were about the value of their friendships.

This extends to famous failures of friendship as well, such as between the nineteenth-century American philosophers and authors Ralph Waldo Emerson and Henry David Thoreau. Emerson and Thoreau's relationship was intense, close, and tumultuous, concluding darkly at the younger Thoreau's funeral when Emerson "eulogized" him by saying that "instead of engineering for all America," Thoreau was really just "the captain of a huckleberry party."[26] As the saying goes, with friends like that, who needs enemies?

But something has changed. Despite being a central topic in the ethical and societal reflections of all the great thinkers of the past, friendship almost entirely disappeared from philosophical discussion in the nineteenth and twentieth centuries. In modern professional philosophy, friendship goes the way of all of the practical and life-shaping aspects of ancient philosophy; that is, it disappears.

As we have seen, philosophy instead focuses on abstractions of epistemology, language, and ideals; and even ethics is largely depersonalized and disconnected from daily life and practice. Immanuel Kant's deontological approach to ethics comes to dominate, wherein ethics is not about *the person in relationships* but about impartial universalizable laws, about producing the greatest good for human beings in general. There is no room in such an ethical construction for the ancient ideas of friendship that focused on personal, preferential relationships between individuals who shared affinities and the pursuit of personal wholeness and virtue.[27]

The chicken-and-egg relationship between leading thinkers and social practice is just as mysterious as that old metaphor—which came first is impossible to discern, but they both affect and create the other. This causation enigma applies to what happened in the twentieth century with friendships in the West. The disappearance of friendship from philosophical discussion corresponds to the diminishment and shift away from its intentional practice in the late modern period. It's impossible to know which came first, but there was definitely a loss. People continued to have close friends but the cultural expectations and habits regarding friendship have shrunk in noticeable ways.

Benjamin Myers and Wes Hill identify several myths that Western culture has imbibed that have diminished our understanding and practice of friendship. One myth is what may be called the Freud Factor. Sigmund Freud's largely-discredited-but-still-lingering psychology promulgated the suspicion that all relationships have at their base an eroticism (usually frustrated), meaning that "the desire for sex is the secret truth of every relationship."[28] As a result, the notion of intense, affectionate same-gender relationships now have cast over them the shadow of suspicion that there must be something more going on than mere friendship. In her research about boy friendships and the "crisis of connection," Niobe Way found that a major shift occurred in the kind of close friendships early-teen boys experience. Later-teen boys nearly all abandoned these formerly intimate, connected, nonsexual relationships with other boys for fear of being suspected of being gay.[29]

Contemporary movies like *I Love You, Man!*, cultural jokes, and the bullying of homosexuals all reveal the way our culture has come to negatively construe strong same-gender relationships. At a recent men-only weekend intensive I attended, there was one exercise where every one of the sixty-plus men had removed their shirts—only shirts! The awkward feelings evoked were addressed thoughtfully, recalling that throughout human history this seminakedness (and more) would have been entirely normal in athletic events, religious rituals, public bathing, and when warriors gathered for war. But today men feel remarkably uncomfortable in this kind of situation. Even with this thoughtful articulation of what we were feeling, several flittering jokes were made afterward between friends about how they weren't gay. All of this reveals a major cultural shift that reflects and extends the loss of same-gender relationships that people had before our culture become so eroticized. In C. S. Lewis's wonderful book *The Four Loves*, he already found it necessary in pre–World War II England to defend the nonsexual nature of close male or female relationships.[30] How much more today.

A comparable problem occurs today with friendships between the genders. As Aimee Byrd talks about in her book *Why Can't We Be Friends?*, the *When Harry Met Sally* factor makes us believe that men and women can't experience close friendships, because "the sex part always gets in the way." The habit of avoiding male-female friendships out of fear of impurity (maybe especially for Christians) damages and denigrates both women and men. We view each other not as brothers and sisters, with value to add to our lives and good things to share, but only as people we might accidentally sleep with.[31] This is another example of the damage of the Freud Factor.

Another cultural assumption that has negatively affected the depth of friendships today is the newfound idea that marriage will meet all of one's social, relational, and emotional needs. Though romantic songs and Pinterest-posted wedding sentiments often express that one is "marrying my best friend" and that all needs are now met through one's spouse, this is a very new hypothesis in human history and one that is questionable as an operating assumption or expectation. Wes Hill notes that as recently as the Victorian era, society had a rich panoply of same-gender relationships and associations that were central to societal and personal health.[32] Marriage (even understood romantically) was but one such relationship, and not the primary one for one's emotional needs. Going back further into antiquity we see this was decidedly not the presumption. As scholar Craig Williams notes when discussing ancient Roman ideas:

> Marriage was not traditionally described as the unique locus of a special type of love between two individuals: that was the function of, precisely, friendship. Indeed, there is a noticeable tendency through the Latin textual tradition to idealize friendship more highly than marriage, and in doing so to use imagery

familiar from later celebrations of romantic love and marriage. The motif of the friend as *alter ego*, for example, corresponds to modern idealizing of one's spouse or partner as "my other half" (or the even more self-effacing "better half"), yet nowhere in surviving texts is it applied to husbands and wives.[33]

○ ○ ○ ○

So we have seen that relationships of various sorts were a regular part of the philosophical diet in the ancient world. And why wouldn't they be? Since ancient philosophy focused on helping people see and be in the world in a certain way that would provide flourishing, it would necessarily involve direction on how to structure and curate human relationships of every kind—marital, familial, friendly, and political.

Christianity's
Renewed Relationships

nn Patchett's novel *Bel Canto* tells the dramatic story of a South American political hostage situation. Inspired originally by the events of the 1996–1997 Japanese embassy hostage crisis in Lima, Peru, Patchett combines opera, violence, politics, and love in this poignant novelized narrative. But it's not a spy thriller or political piece. It's a well-paced and beautiful story about relationships.

A group of terrorists break into the vice president's home on the night of a special event being held for a wealthy Japanese businessman. Many important figures are present for the party, including a famous American opera singer, who is there to entertain them. The terrorists had hoped to capture the president for political reasons, but their plan goes awry when they discover that he is not there. Instead, these young terrorists find themselves in a long-term hostage situation with this unexpected group of international people, hoping for ransoms and freedom.

In this pressure-cooker situation of multiple languages, personalities, and real human needs, the people do what humans always do—they form relationships. Over the course of the long besiegement, unexpected and deep relationships develop between the businessman and the opera singer, as well the translator and one of the young terrorist women. The novel is as beautifully told as it is insightful into the deepest of human experiences—relationships of all kinds: companionship, friendship, romance, mentoring, and social. All of this can be described under the banner of *bel canto*, "beautiful singing."

○ ○ ○ ○

"Beautiful singing" is an apt description of Christianity's vision for the goodness of relationships in God's created and redeemed world. In the New Testament, the apostles are positing a philosophical vision for what all kinds of relationships can and should look like. In this the biblical writers are consciously entering into a dialogue with their surrounding cultures, particularly the Greco-Roman world. As we have seen, the philosophers had a vision for the importance of all kinds of relationships and how they should be structured to make society flourish. The Bible does too.

The Christian philosophy's vision is rooted in God's creation of the world and consummated in the incarnation of the God-man Jesus into this world. Jesus's life and teaching can fairly be described as a re-forming and renewing of all kinds of relationships—between God and humanity and between humans of every language, ethnicity, gender, and class. By asking the Bible questions that center on relationships—questions that are helpfully guided by comparing the same questions in Greco-Roman philosophy—we gain a particularly important line of sight into Christianity's philosophy of life.

○ ○ ○ ○

What does the Bible have to say about household relationships? We saw in the previous chapter that marriage and family were important topics of discussion in Greek and Roman philosophy. This is because of the inescapable fact that the most intimate and society-foundational relationships are those that create and sustain families. The philosophy of both the Old and New Testaments argues the same.

In the very beginning of the biblical story we meet a pair of humans who need relationship with each other. It was not good for Adam to be alone. Eve provides necessary completion, help, and support, as well as the only means of procreation. Neither Adam nor Eve are fully sufficient by themselves, because together in their male and female distinction they reflect the image of the invisible God. "So God created mankind in his own image, in the image of God he created them; male and female he created them" (Gen. 1:27). At the core of the biblical vision of humanity is a recognition of both distinction between humans (genderwise and individually) and their mutual interdependence. Male and female humans together complete their respective roles as vice-regents in God's kingdom creation. Male and female together are the image of God.

From this foundational, intimate relationship comes the family structure upon which all of society is built. In the opening chapters of Genesis we see that the ups and downs, the victories and the failures of humanity are all tied into relationships. That is, the primordial story of the Bible is not one of man versus nature, or any of the other primary literary tropes. Such typical master stories *are* there in the Bible—the quest, rags to riches, voyage and return, and so on. But what primarily drives the earliest stories in the Bible are relationships. Relationships between God and humanity and relationships between humans are the heart of the vision. Adam and Eve's children are jealous of, fight, kill, fall in love with, defend, and revenge one another. It's all about relationships, good and bad. It is no accident that the super-condensed primordial history culminates with

157

the organization of the world into tribes or families, explaining how everything came into being via familial descendants (Gen. 11).

The rest of the story of the Old Testament follows one of these families: Abraham's. The millennia of twists and turns that is the history of the Hebrew people is again a story of relationships, sometimes beautiful, sometimes distorted and destructive. Once God reveals his covenantal instructions through Moses, it is families that form the structure of Israel's society. It is through the family that God's instructions are passed down, thereby presevering society and faithfulness to God. The foundational Shema (Deut. 6:4–6) is immediately followed by instructions to teach this to one's children and build the truth about God into the very structure of one's house (6:7–9).

The high point of the story of Israel is under its greatest king, David. In ways that are remarkably parallel to other societies, the kingship of Israel is understood simultaneously as sonship and as fatherhood. The good king is the son of God, his heir. And consequently, the good king is the representative father of the people—the provider, the shepherd, the protector, the sage who leads with great wisdom. Thus, the good society is structured like a good household.

oooo

When we turn to the New Testament, we see the same vision for the foundational structure of the household relationships. But in earliest Christianity this is made even more explicit as a dialogue with its surrounding Greco-Roman world. One of the most obvious parallels between the New Testament and its surrounding philosophical world is in the standard usage of "household codes." Household codes were short, bullet-point-like instructions to different members of a domestic domain, giving direction on what each person should do in their role to promote virtue and flourishing for everyone. These were standard fare in ancient moral teaching, because they were so practical and relevant. Husbands, wives, children, and servants were all given specific, direct moral instruction. Examples in the New Testament are manifold, including the listings in Ephesians 5:22–6:9; Colossians 3:18–4:1; 1 Peter 2:13–3:7; with hints of this kind of teaching in other texts as well (e.g., 1 John 2:12–14).

These kinds of instructions for the ongoing stable life of people in the church make an important contribution to the Christian whole-life philosophy. They are yet another example of how Christianity is more than a religion. It is a deeply sophisticated philosophy.

In these Christian household codes the most striking observation is how much value and worth is put on *every* member of the household. There are specific instructions given to people in different roles—husbands, wives, children, parents, servants, household heads—but these are always functional differences, not differences in worth. That is, Christianity's philosophy is that even though people should function in particular ways for the sake of the harmony of the whole, *every person is equal in worth and value*. Thus, Christianity teaches people to think of other Christians as *brothers and sisters*, regardless of their status, success, or role in the household. This stands in contrast to many other philosophies in the ancient world that devalued women, children, and servants as being actually worth less than others. Christianity's radical egalitarianism of worth is remarkable relative to its surrounding culture.

So the Christian household codes are seeking to reshape the Christian community with its distinct philosophy of relationships. But these codes are rather tame and conservative compared to the way family relationships are treated in the Gospels. In the Gospels we see Jesus affirming the foundational structure of family by using household metaphors. But Jesus is also radically disruptive. Jesus simultaneously asserts the centrality of family structures and redefines them at the core.

One of the most striking examples of this comes to us in the story in Matthew 12:46–50. Jesus's mother and brothers attempt to break through the massive crowds to reach their now-famous relative. They are distraught and probably seeking to bring him back home. And they have good reason to be concerned. This formerly mild-mannered son and brother of theirs recently abandoned the family carpentry business to become a charismatic, wandering prophet and exorcist, and he kicked off his ministry with a forty-day foodless sojourn in the desert. And now, rumor has it that the religious leaders are planning to kill him because he is so disruptive. This has gone too far.

Jesus's response to his family's seeking him is culture-overturning—"Who is my mother, and who are my brothers?" he says (Matt. 12:48). And then he stretches out his hands toward his disciples and proclaims, "Here are my mother and my brothers. For whoever does the will of my Father in heaven is my brother and sister and mother" (12:49–50).[1]

This is quite a statement. It is the articulation of what he has already been showing with his actions—calling disciples away from their families' business and livelihood, and even temporarily from their wives, as we know at least in the case of Peter, who has a mother-in-law (Matt. 4:18–22). Jesus is disrupting normal family relations and expectations and forming them in a new way.

He anticipates the familial disruption and even conflict this will cause. When instructing his new disciples on what life as a follower of Jesus will look like, he says, "Brother will betray brother to death, and a father his child; children will rebel against their parents and have them put to death" (Matt. 10:21).

If this isn't disruptive enough, we see Jesus instruct his rag-tag band of disciples, made up of all kinds of people—tax

collectors, prostitutes, fishermen, lepers, political revolutionaries—to call each other and to treat each other as "brothers" and "sisters" (Matt. 5:22–24; 7:4; 18:15–22, 35). To put
the cherry on the top of this family-deserting dessert, Jesus
chooses to celebrate the national, family-centered Jewish holiday of Passover not with his biological family but with his new
grab bag of disciples. He calls them to leave their families for
the holiday too. This feels like a group of college kids living
on dad's dime deciding to not go home for Christmas but
spurn their families and rent a house together in Miami for
the holidays.

The point of all of this is not disruption for disruption's
sake but an intentional redefinition of family based on unity
in Christ. In the Bible and throughout Christian theology and
practice, the Christian whole-life philosophy has been remarkably strong in its affirmation of the central role that marriage,
parenting, and household relationships play—so much so that
being a good household manager, father, and husband is one
of the requirements for leadership in the church, with failure
in this area being a disqualifier (Titus 1:5–9).

At the same time, the Christian's primary identity is in relationship to other Christians, their true and lasting nonbio-
logical family. Whatever family is lost now will be more than
appropriately restored. As Jesus said, "Truly I tell you, at the
renewal of all things, when the Son of Man sits on his glorious throne, you who have followed me will also sit on twelve
thrones, judging the twelve tribes of Israel. And everyone who
has left houses or brothers or sisters or father or mother or
children or fields for my sake will receive a hundred times as
much and will inherit eternal life" (Matt. 19:28–29). Jesus is a
subversive philosopher of family relationships. Thus, there is a
rich and nuanced philosophy of family that pervades the Bible
and shapes the Christian life.

○ ○ ○ ○

The "separation of church and state" is such a basic presumption of modern Western civilization that it can be shocking to learn what a relatively new idea this is in the long scope of human society. Separating religion from societal structures and government values was an "enlightened" idea that arose only in the modern period. Separation of church and state in the Enlightenment was an understandable reaction to the worst kind of overlapping of religious ideals and government in the seventeenth century. Political and religious interests together swung a bloody broadsword across Europe for much of the century. That's bad. But the overreactionary solution that politics and religion could or should remain entirely separate is as naive as it is impossible.

This modern assumption of a separation of religion and politics blinds modern Christians from discerning how central "political" issues are to the Christian philosophy. Let me say it more clearly—the Christian philosophy is thoroughly political. It has much to say about societal relationships.

When we look at how the New Testament engages politics, we can see that it does so with the same kinds of questions that ancient philosophers spoke about:

- How should people relate to the nation/culture/ government?
- How should Christianity's interior society be structured?

What does the Christian philosophy have to say about these two big issues?

○ ○ ○ ○

The Old Testament is a deeply political document. It is a political story about real people doing what people do—building societies that grow into nations with interests and inevitable governmental structures. After all, the story of Israel is a story of a kingdom. It is God's kingdom manifested through a particular people with the end goal being the establishment of God's reign upon all the earth.

This story starts with the creation account, with Adam and Eve depicted as vice-regents, sub-king and sub-queen, put in charge of God's royal garden. Much of the long and winding story between this glorious beginning and the full establishment of the kingdom under David is a tale of decline and failure. That is, in reading the stories of Abraham, Isaac, Jacob, and Moses it would be easy to forget that the whole point of the story is God's kingdom coming from heaven to earth. There is so much darkness and sin woven into all of these stories that the bread crumbs of the trail leading to God's kingdom can be few, far between, and easy to miss. But they are there.

Repeatedly throughout the Old Testament God is called King, and we find many references to God reigning and ruling (e.g., Exod. 15:18; 1 Chron. 28:5; Pss. 5:2; 10:16; 24:7; 44:4; 47:2; 68:24; 95:3; 103:19; 145:1–13). And these are found at crucial places—such as in the worship of God when he showed up in particular ways. One foundational example is when God rescued his people from Egypt and established a covenant with them. In joyful thanksgiving, the people sing that "the LORD reigns forever and ever" (Exod. 15:18) even as they stand on the banks of the Red Sea that has just swallowed up the warriors and chariots of the great king of Egypt. Then through Moses God leads the people up to Mount Sinai and makes a political and moral contract with them about how to honor him as King and how to live with each other for the purpose of shalom/flourishing.

The apex of Israel's story is the establishment of God's kingdom under his appointed earthly son, King David. This kingdom of God on earth takes one more step forward in glory under David's son, Solomon, only to be cracked, splintered, and eventually swallowed up by surrounding nations in the subsequent generations. The writings of the prophets that follow and which consume the rest of Israel's story and literature are hopeful and forward looking. The prophets repeatedly speak of a particular hope—that God is going to return to finally and fully establish his good and just reign on earth.

This hope, in the language of the great prophet Isaiah, is the "gospel." It is the "good news" that God is going to comfort those who are mourning, forgive the sins of the repentant, bring peace between people and creation itself (such that even a lion and a lamb can hang out), deliver people from bondage and oppression, uplift the poor and humble, and rid the world of evil people, war, hatred, and death. This great vision and hope is stated succinctly in Isaiah 52:7:

> How beautiful on the mountains
>   are the feet of those who bring good news,
> who proclaim peace,
>   who bring good tidings,
>   who proclaim salvation,
> who say to Zion,
>   "Your God reigns!"

That last line sums it up. The hope for the future Good of the world can be described with those three words—"Your God reigns!"

○ ○ ○ ○

I've said we want to answer the question of what the Christian philosophy says about how to relate to society around us and its governments. This Old Testament story and hope is absolutely essential to comprehend *before* we get to the New

Testament, where we can answer that question. The Old Testament is essential because the message of the New Testament won't make clear sense unless we see it as the fulfillment of the hope and message that God was already speaking for thousands of years. In this last era of human history, God has finally spoken through Jesus, his Son (Heb. 1:1–4). To understand this final word we need to see it *as* the final word to a sentence that began much earlier.

What is that final word from and about Jesus? It is the message that God reigns and he is now finally bringing his kingdom from heaven to earth—through Jesus himself! This is why the first proclamation Jesus made was "Repent, for the kingdom of heaven has come near" (Matt. 4:17). Or to hear it in stereophonic harmony in Luke's version, listen to what Jesus said when he first entered the synagogue and stood up to explain himself:

> The Spirit of the Lord is on me,
>> because he has anointed me
>> to proclaim good news to the poor.
> He has sent me to proclaim freedom for the prisoners
>> and recovery of sight for the blind,
> to set the oppressed free,
>> to proclaim the year of the Lord's favor.
> (Luke 4:18–19)

Intentionally reading from the book of Isaiah, Jesus explains that the long-awaited hope for God's reign is now here through his own life and ministry. Luke tells us, "Then he rolled up the scroll, gave it back to the attendant and sat down. The eyes of everyone in the synagogue were fastened on him. He began by saying to them, 'Today this scripture is fulfilled in your hearing'" (Luke 4:20–21).

○ ○ ○ ○

So the message of Christianity is that God is the true King of the world and that his kingdom has now entered into this world through Jesus. This creates a dilemma, a tension, a potential split of allegiance for Christian kingdom-disciples, who are living in real human kingdoms and nations. So what is the Christian philosophy of how its kingdom citizens are supposed to relate to the visible kingdoms of this world?

The New Testament has a surprising amount to say on this philosophical question, and the answer is nuanced. In the first instance, Christians must understand that they are now citizens of two realms, or two cities, as Augustine would famously describe it—the city of humanity and the city of God.[2] It is necessary to maintain this dual citizenship in wise balance. The Christian should not think of himself or herself as having two comparable allegiances; the Christian is first and last a citizen of the kingdom of heaven, and "no one can serve two masters" (Matt. 6:24).

Yet, as a function of his or her dual citizenship, the Christian must also not neglect the earthly city/kingdom. Neglecting God's kingdom would obviously be disastrous. Yet withdrawing from and neglecting this world would be ceasing to be salt and light (Matt. 5:13–16). This would be a failure of the role that the church plays as God's royal priesthood to the world, proclaiming God's excellencies and inviting people into his love (1 Pet. 2:9). Jesus is the Great High Priest, the agent of healing and light in the world. Thus his disciples are the same, priests in the world who build and bless.

Therefore, the Christian's relationship to the state is one of respectful participation and honor where honor is due (1 Pet. 2:17), praying for even ungodly leaders (1 Tim. 2:1–4). Being a Christian, with allegiance to a different emperor, Jesus Christ the King, does not deny this world and its rulers their proper realm of authority. All such authorities are ultimately in place because the sovereign God has allowed them. So, with wisdom, the Christian philosophy teaches Christians to submit to this God-given authority (Rom. 13:1–7). Jesus himself emphasized that his kingdom is not of this world (John 18:36). This does not mean Christians are free to ignore this world, but instead it frees Christians to relate in a gracious and humble way, knowing their citizenship is ultimately something more and greater and different.

○ ○ ○ ○

The letter to the Christians in Philippi provides another powerful example of how Christians are to relate to the world. Philippi was a prosperous and important Roman city (originally a Greek *polis*) when Paul founded a church there and then later wrote an important letter to them. There are in fact many ways in which the Letter to the Philippians shows Paul's interaction with the philosophies of the day. Philippians is rife with Christian answers to the great philosophical question of how to live well. Paul discusses the importance of enduring suffering well (Phil. 2:19–30), uses language straight from philosophical discussions about the good and honorable things (4:8), and even utilizes images from the Roman games (3:12–16). Paul speaks just like the philosophers of his day in upholding the importance of following examples of virtue (3:17), with Christ as the ultimate example (2:1–11).

But one of the most interesting and subtle ways Paul interacts with the Greco-Roman philosophy is often missed by modern readers: the way he affirms and subverts the idea of "citizenship." Being a virtuous citizen was crucial to the Greek and Roman philosophical discussions. Paul is aware of this and makes this the basis for his instructions for how Christians are to relate to their society.

Near the beginning of the Letter to the Philippians, Paul uses an important and familiar Greek verb, *politeuomai*, the word used to describe living as a citizen and whence we later get our word "politics." Paul encourages the Christians in Philippi to live as good citizens, something they would be used to hearing all the time, but with a crucial additional description—live as good citizens *in such a way that is worthy of the gospel of Christ* (1:27). Near the end of the letter this theme returns with another reference to being a citizen when Paul explains that the Christian's citizenship (*politeuma*) is "in heaven" (3:20). Once again, the nuanced relationship of Christians to the world is on display here. We are to be good citizens while recognizing that our true citizenship is not of this world and is yet to come.

○ ○ ○ ○

In the book of Revelation the new Jerusalem is described as a temple. The city of God descending to earth is given, weirdly it seems, very specific physical dimensions (Rev. 21:15–17). When we read these specified dimensions in light of the rest of Holy Scripture, we realize that the new Jerusalem is being described exactly like the temple of God. It is a city—the city—where God himself dwells and from which the light of the world emanates, with Jesus enthroned as its Son-King (21:22–27).

Scholar Peter Leithart explores what this means. The church is a temple-city, the place where the Triune God dwells and from which the reign of God will rightly go from being localized to universal. This temple-city, this worshiping *polis*, is a real, visible community comprising all who wear the robes of the people of God. The church now is the future city that has entered the present, waiting for its full form and structure when Jesus consummates the new creation hope.

Because the church is the presence of God's city on earth now, this means it is inherently political. As the temple-city of God it "exists to transform and renew human societies, inside and out, top to bottom."[3] This is what a healthy and thriving city does—welcome and expand and develop in life-giving ways. How much more the city of God!

The New Testament authors give unmistakable hints that this is how we are to think of the church by describing it with terms that come straight from ancient political theory.[4] Let's take two obvious descriptors—*ekklēsia* (which we translate "church") and *koinōnia* ("fellowship"). The biblical authors' choice to use the Greek word *ekklēsia* is significant (Matt. 16:18; 18:17; 1 Cor. 1:2; Eph. 1:22; Rev. 1:4). It was already used in the Greek translation of the Old Testament to describe the assembled gathering of God's people. The New Testament follows suit. The writers and translators of both Testaments knew what they were doing when they adopted this famous Greek word. No Greek-reading person would miss the implication of *ekklēsia*, which is central in Aristotle. In Greek political theory the citizens gathered together in unison so that they could live and rule well, knowing that the flourishing of the city depended on this unity. The collective wisdom of the *ekklēsia* is necessary for the Good Life. This is what the *ekklēsia* was in Aristotle, and this is what it means in the Old Testament and New Testament as well. Closely related is the term *koinōnia*, which described the community of the city-state, the people who make it up and are acting together for the Good (1 John 1:7). To have *koinōnia* is to participate in the common Good of the society. Once again, it is no accident that the church adopts this term to describe itself. The church has its own political philosophy.

This situating of the Christian philosophy into the context of ancient discussions of the *polis* makes the church's engagement with the world real and palpable. It would have made perfect sense to the earliest Christians, but we need to rediscover the implications for us today. The church as the city-temple is not to have a fifty-foot impregnable protective wall built around it, with its citizens holed up and fearful, listening only to recordings produced on Christian labels and reading only books written by approved Christian authors. No, Jesus died to break down the dividing wall between Jews and gentiles and to form a new human race that comes from men and women from every nation, ethnicity, and background (Eph. 2:11–22). And this heavenly city isn't static. The city-temple church is, as Leithart says, "not merely *placed* in the world, among the cities and nations of men. God established His city among the cities of men to *redeem* those human cities. Jesus commissioned the church to disciple nations. He established His city to engage in an urban renewal project."[5] The Christian philosophy teaches that the church is an outward-directed, gracious political reality.

○ ○ ○ ○

That's the outward look—how Christians should relate to the outside world. The Christian philosophy also has much to say about the inward set of relationships—how Christians should organize their interior society. Every culture has their own vision of how society should be structured. In the ancient world the Persians, Greeks, Romans, and others were conscious of their philosophical differences on this important matter. The Greeks called this the *politeia*, the unwritten contract of how society should be put together and what would be valued or devalued. Today Americans do things a certain way that is different than the French, the English, or the Chinese. Narrowing down even more, society is structured quite differently in New Orleans, Boston, Los Angeles, and the other LA (Lower Alabama).

The church is also a structured society, described as an *ekklēsia* and *koinōnia*. But we often don't think this way. Internal church societal relationships are a prime example of our modern tendency to think of Christianity as only a religion, not a whole-life philosophy, as vertical but not horizontal.

Peter Leithart once again is insightful on this issue. He notes that we often think and talk about the church as an invisible and spiritual community. While this is true in one sense, the fact is that the people of the church form a visible and physical community of real flesh-and-blood humans with a whole range of relationships. The redemption that Jesus brings into the world isn't an escape from this world or from other people in relationship. Rather, "Redemption is becoming a member of a new society of which God's Spirit is the animating breath and of which Jesus Christ is head."[6]

To be a Christian is to be called into a new community of being-redeemed people. The Roman Catholic tradition has famously proclaimed that there is no salvation apart from the church (the *ekklēsia*). By this they mean their particular tradition of the church, with its sacraments, priests, and traditions. As a Protestant, I would kindly disagree with some of those specifics. But in another sense this claim is profoundly true. There is no salvation that is free separate from entry into the church. That is, to be saved, to be a Christian, to be a disciple is precisely to enter the universal church of all true believers, which means *to enter into a new society*. Or as the Gospels typically articulate it, to enter into the kingdom of God.

○ ○ ○ ○

So if being a Christian means entering into a new society, what does this society look like? Jesus and the New Testament regularly paint a picture of what the true *politeia* modeled on God's kingdom should be. Christian teaching is a vision that resocializes people's values and habits, that creates a new community of people, a new covenant people who will live together in love and serve as a model for the world of God himself. This is a sophisticated philosophy of relationships.

The reason Jesus was so infuriating to both religious and government leaders was not because he was taking up arms and trying to overthrow governments but because his radical teachings were so subversive to society. Jesus was subversive because he sought to reform all sorts of relationships. In his teachings and actions, Jesus continually subverted fundamental values of both Jewish and Greco-Roman society. His model and his teaching shaped a group of disciples who came to see and be in the world in a very different way. They in turn made disciples themselves. Societal change that comes through relationships is unstoppable.

Within only a few decades this new way of seeing and being in the world had spread throughout the Roman Empire and beyond. This was not just a message of doctrinal truth but a philosophy that taught people to relate to each other in particular ways. As Jesus said, the world will know that people are his disciples *by their love for one another* (John 13:35), not their adopting of a set of doctrines. Christian discipleship changed people's values, sensibilities, hopes, imaginations, habits, and virtues. There is nothing more dangerous and unsettling to society than that!

We see this new *politeia* explicitly in many texts, such as the following:

- Matthew 18—A picture of life together that focuses on living in relationships of superabundant forgiveness, with the "little ones" being protected and valued. Those who are unwilling to forgive others are excluded from this society of Jesus.

- Acts 4:32—Christians sharing their goods with one another in an alternative subcommunity of care. This financial service to each other crosses ethnic and class lines, creating a new community around Jesus.

- 1 Corinthians 11:17–34—The great symbol of Christian practice is a shared table, a communion table where Christians of all races, social classes, genders, educational levels, and incomes gather together without divisions between them, as one people united as a new family through Jesus Christ.
- 1 Corinthians 12–14—The church as a society where the Holy Spirit is actively guiding and empowering people to speak and teach, all centered in radical love for each other.
- Galatians 6:1–10—A society where people bear each other's burdens, helping those who have failed and providing for those who lead and teach well, doing good to everyone, especially those in the household of faith.
- Ephesians 5:21–6:9—The household codes that instruct individuals in relating to each other in mutual love and honoring submission. In the Christian community, children, wives, and servants/slaves are valued as equal citizens who should be honored as brothers and sisters.

These are but a few examples. Every book of the New Testament contains instructions for the new Christian *politeia*, life together. It is entirely natural that the following centuries of early Christianity continue to use *politeia* to describe Jesus's teachings. These Christians understood something we have forgotten—Christianity is a deeply intentional and practical philosophy of relationships.

○ ○ ○ ○

Like many other Americans over the last fifty years, I've made the pilgrimage to sit with friends at "The Bird and Baby." This is the official unofficial name for the Oxford pub The Eagle and Child, the longtime meeting place for the now-famous writing group the Inklings. The goal of this Anglophiliac pilgrimage is to find and sit at the little back table under the same low ceiling that hung over J. R. R. Tolkien, C. S. Lewis, Owen Barfield, Charles Williams, and others as they discussed each other's writings.

As told in Lewis's spiritual autobiography, it was on a walk in nearby Magdalen College with one of these committed friends, Tolkien, that he experienced his conversion to the Christian faith. From that group of friends came not only Lewis's mythical Narnia stories but also Tolkien's famous three-part epic, *The Lord of the Rings*. Undoubtedly encouraged by his own experience of friendship, Tolkien wove into his mythical tour de force the beauty and goodness of friendship as a moral theme. Frodo Baggins's long and dangerous journey to "unmake" the ring of power would have ended in failure many times over if it were not for his faithful friend Sam Gamgee. Sam, the model of a virtuous friend, knows no equal in literature.

Nothing is wasted or thoughtless in Tolkien's elaborate fictional world. This includes the central role that friendship plays in holding together the whole long "there and back again" journey story. Like so many other themes in *The Lord of the Rings* (such as gardening and trees), Tolkien is seeking to recapture a crucial element of what it means to be human and live well—friendship. Even though there is conspicuously no religion in the Middle Earth universe, Tolkien's deeply orthodox Catholic commitments undergird every page. This, combined with his love for the premodern world, means Tolkien models a deeply committed Christian philosophy of friendship.

○ ○ ○ ○

We saw in our discussion of Greco-Roman relationships, maybe surprisingly, that friendship was at the nuclear core and the mountain heights of the ancient philosophies. Especially with

Aristotle and continuing throughout the tradition, friendship is not secondary or superfluous; it is a moral reality. Friendship is, as Hugh Black describes it, "the flower of Ethics and the root of Politics," referring to Aristotle's two greatest works. Friendship unites the personal and the communal aspects of what it means to be human, simultaneously the chamber in which our virtues are formed and the bedrock upon which a flourishing society is built.[7]

With this philosophical air filling the lungs of both Jews and gentiles in the first century, Jesus's actions and articulations regarding friendship make a lot more sense. We might even say that when we put Jesus's activities and talk regarding friendship in his historical and philosophical context, it goes from being black and white on the page to Technicolor, even 3D. But because of our own contemporary loss of intentional reflection on friendship, we have lacked ears to hear and eyes to see the central role that friendship plays in the philosophy of Holy Scripture. But it is there.

Abraham was called the friend of God in Isaiah 41:8 (repeated in James 2:23), a lofty claim worthy of his status as the patriarch of God's chosen people. Likewise, the great prophet-leader Moses alone spoke to God directly "as one speaks to a friend" (Exod. 33:11), resulting in a glory-shined countenance.

When we think of friendship in the Old Testament, there are two pairs that especially come to mind—Ruth and Naomi, David and Jonathan—who, interestingly, are closely related and both central to God's kingdom on earth. Ruth and Naomi were not of the same age or ethnicity, but they provide a model of an exemplary kind of thick and rich friendship.[8] Naomi was a Hebrew who found herself a widow and bereaved of two sons in the foreign land of Moab. Ruth was one of her daughters-in-law, a Moabite, who models the loyalty of true friendship. When Naomi plans to head back to Bethlehem, she tries to dismiss her two daughters-in-law. Orpah does as she is bidden, but Ruth will not be dissuaded and utters these famous words of friendship—"Where you go I will go, and where you stay I will stay. Your people will be my people and your God my God. Where you die I will die, and there I will be buried" (Ruth 1:16–17). The result of this kind of radical loyalty is a change in history itself—through the twists and turns of the story, Ruth becomes the great-grandmother of King David.

David likely knew the marvelous story about his Moabite great-grandmother's loyalty and model. But regardless of how aware he was, David himself provides what is the greatest biblical example of deep and loyal friendship. The road to David's eventual glorious reign was filled with chasms of pain and despair. The previously appointed King Saul proved to be unfaithful to God and tried to kill David. In the transition time of Saul's demise and David's rise, there was great conflict and animosity from the existing king toward this young, charismatic man David. In a plot twist as creative as any Hollywood screenplay, Saul's own son Jonathan proves to be the crucial player in the ultimate rise and success of the new king, David, who would replace his own father (and therefore himself) as the next king.

David and Jonathan had a loving, deep, committed friendship. They were, as we would say today, "kindred spirits" who became fast friends. Their friendship rivals any in Greek and Roman literature and would have made Aristotle proud. Jonathan describes it in ways that would become very common in the Greek tradition—in David he found "another self." Jonathan made a covenant of loyalty with David because he "loved him as himself" (1 Sam. 18:1–3). A few in our contemporary age have tried to interpret David and Jonathan's relationship as homosexual. But such erotic interpretations of their friendship reveal more about these interpreters' cultural situatedness than they do about friendships in the ancient world. The Freud Factor strikes again. David and Jonathan are clearly being presented as models of what most humans have always valued—committed same-gender relationships that provide meaning and flourishing in life that is much deeper and wider than mere sexuality.

Most importantly, the friendships of both Ruth and Naomi and of David and Jonathan center on the beautiful biblical idea of *hesed*, often translated "covenant faithfulness" or "steadfast love." This central biblical concept is the primary way in which God relates to his creatures. *Hesed* is a core characteristic of who God himself is—he is faithful, loving, making committed covenantal relationships with people whom he chooses. It is no accident that this way that God relates to humanity is the ultimate model for how humans can and should relate to each other. Both marriage and friendship are places where *hesed* is the glue, the framework, the heart of human relationships. The Hebrew philosophy of friendship is *hesed*.

○ ○ ○ ○

With the beautiful singing of Ruth, Naomi, David, Jonathan, and God himself in our ears, we can turn the page of music to the New Testament. Here we find that Jesus regularly sounds notes of friendship, using the biblical and the contemporary Greco-Roman language of friendship to explain his own relationship to his disciples.

As we have seen, Plato, Aristotle, and Epicurus weren't philosophers on the model of today's scholar. They weren't tenured professors who spent most of their time alone reading and writing, coming out of their office occasionally to teach. They weren't people whose personal lives, religion, and physical exercise were separate from their scholarship. No, the ancient philosophers lived an integrated life together in a school with "friends" committed to the same vision and purpose. I put "friends" in quotation marks because the ancient sense of friends was much deeper and more intentional that the diluted sense of that word today. Plato's Academy, Aristotle's Lyceum, and Epicurus's Garden were places of discipleship where a community of like-minded people gathered around a sage to learn to see and be in the world in a particular way. Because of this they called each other friends.

The Greek and Jewish tradition of discipleship as a collection of friends committed to learn from a sage helps Jesus the Disciple Maker make sense. Jesus's mode throughout the Gospels is to call people to leave their current way of seeing and being in the world and to follow him. This following of Jesus can be described as people taking his yoke upon them (Matt. 11:28–30), as putting their hand to his plow and not looking back (Luke 9:62), as being *with* him so they could learn his ways. In other words, Jesus sets up a three-year mobile philosophical school to train disciples so that when he returns to the Father, his disciples can continue to live in the ways he taught them and make more communities of disciples all over the world (Matt. 28:18–20).

This is why Jesus calls his disciples "friends" and speaks with them in the way one only speaks with a friend—in complete and open honesty. The Greeks called this bold honesty *parrhēsia*, "frankness of speech," which is only used with trusted friends.[9] Romans like Seneca spoke the same way: "Ponder for a long time whether you shall admit a given person to your friendship; but when you have decided to admit him, welcome him with all your heart and soul. Speak as boldly with him as with yourself."[10]

The apostle Paul also speaks this same way when appealing to the heavily philosophical Corinthians, so that they recognize his sincerity. He thinks of believers as *friends* in this deepest sense and therefore he speaks frankly with them (2 Cor. 7:4).

And so does Jesus. To adopt the Christian philosophy is to become a group of true friends.

○ ○ ○ ○

In recent years many professors have been asked to imagine how they would sum up their teaching if they had just one final lecture to give. This is called the "Last Lecture" exercise. This took on a deeper level of poignancy for the young Carnegie Mellon professor Randy Pausch, who gave his "Last Lecture" after he found out about his terminal pancreatic cancer. In his 2007 talk that was turned into a *New York Times* bestseller, Pausch spoke about "Really Achieving Your Childhood Dreams." His words are helpful, emphasizing that ultimately the goal is to live life well. But what makes the lecture so powerful is the impending death that hangs over the whole scene. Death gives a focus and weightiness to words.

There is no weightier and more focusing moment in Jesus's own life than his last night with his beloved disciples. At this crucial moment in the Gospel of John, when Jesus is preparing for his death and departure from this world, Jesus gives his final instructions to his disciples. The Upper Room Discourse of John 13–17 is chock-full, focusing mostly on the necessity of the disciples' love for one another and the promise of Jesus's continual presence with them through the coming Holy Spirit. Up until this point in John, Jesus has spoken in ambiguous, deeply figurative ways that have left his opponents, the crowds, and even the disciples rather confused about what he was saying. But now, finally, Jesus speaks with frankness (*parrhēsia*) with his chosen disciples, his friends (John 16:25–30).

Popular speaker Jim Rohn has observed that in many ways we are the combination of the five people we spend the most time with. As we are always becoming and shifting in our attitudes, practices, and habits, whom we spend the most time with is a major factor in who we are becoming. Jesus gathered around himself friends to shape them to be like himself. Intentionally, as the Son of God incarnate, he formed a philosophical school centered on his wisdom so that he might transform people to become like himself.

One of the most striking places this vision becomes enfleshed is at the Christian practice of the Lord's Table, or Communion. In Greek and Roman cultures, educated men often gathered together for long banquets. The postmeal part was called the symposium (Greek) or convivium (Roman). At the symposium the guests reclined on cushions, ate and drank, and discussed all manner of philosophical matters, often especially love and gender. The symposium is a gathering of philosophical friends who (partly tongue-loosened by the strong wine) would speak frankly with each other in this special environment. It was a place and time of equality among friends.

Early Christians also had a friend-gathered meal and postmeal discussion of great philosophical truths. But Christians consciously subverted this cultural practice in a crucial way. In the Christian symposium, drunkenness was discouraged and the radical Christian philosophy about the equality of all humans was the goal. That is, the Lord's Table became the premier place to manifest Christianity's philosophical belief that real and equal friendship was possible across races, genders, ethnicities, social classes, and educational levels. All Christians are friends. It was a failure on this precise issue that made the apostle Paul address the practice of the Table in 1 Corinthians 11. The beautiful culture-subversiveness of Christianity is seen in how it takes the idea of friendship and transforms it into a friendship that is centered in the universal image of God in all humans with Jesus as the Perfect and Second Adam. To be a Christian is to be a friend of God, shaped and transformed through a group of friends.

○○○○

Modern sitcom plots often depend on groups of friends. Some of the most popular shows in the last twenty years include collections of four to six adult friends who navigate the complexities of life together—shows like *Seinfeld*, *How I Met Your Mother*, and, of course, *Friends*. These shows depict friendships, but ones that have a heavy dose of TV unreality to them and nothing more than an ambiguous and tenuous bond. There is a pleasure to be found in such affinity-based groups of friends, but they typically depict childless and familyless people living commitmentless lives free from pain, suffering, or even the bored mundaneness of a regular life.

The Christian philosophy's vision for relationships includes pleasurable friendships, certainly, but something richer, more real, and more comprehensive. Christianity is a kingdom, a stratified and diverse series of relationships between leaders, followers, friends, parents, and children, between people of diverse ethnicities, races, and socioeconomic levels. All of these people whose Father is God are now called brothers and sisters. Christians are fellow citizens of an empire whose King is Jesus, parts of one body whose head is Christ. The Christian philosophy teaches that all believers are simultaneously family and friends.

But unlike sitcom relationships, the reality is that our lives are broken through sin—the brokenness not only of sin that has corrupted creation itself but also of personal acts of evil, foolishness, and harm. Thus, the Christian philosophy's vision for relationships within God's kingdom is not naive or idealistic. Instead, Christianity understands that we are wounded through relationships and will only find healing through relationships. This starts with a relationship with God the Father, made possible to all people through the incarnation of Jesus

181

the Son, now applied and empowered through the abiding Holy Spirit at work in the world.

On the basis of this love from God and love for God comes the greatest relational command in Holy Scripture—love for one another. Whatever else may be said about the nature and structure of Christian relationships, *love for one another* is the distinguishing mark. It is through Christians' relationships of love for one another—not their moral stances, not their doctrinal accuracy in minutiae—that the outside world will know what it means to be a Christian (John 13:35).

Internally, this same love for others is the mark that believers truly love God. As the first letter from the apostle John says it: "Whoever claims to love God yet hates a brother or sister is a liar. For whoever does not love their brother and sister, whom they have seen, cannot love God, whom they have not seen. And he has given us this command: Anyone who loves God must also love their brother and sister" (1 John 4:20–21).

This intrakingdom love is manifested in helping each other with practical needs (1 John 3:17–18), in exercising patience and kindness, in keeping no record of wrongs (1 Cor. 13:4–7), and in forgiving those who wrong us (Matt. 18:21–35). These loving relationships are the beautiful kingdom anthem of the Christian philosophy. This is a philosophy of restored relationships or *bel canto*, beautiful singing.

BEING
HUMAN
AND HAPPY

Humans, We Have a Problem

While standing in line at my neighborhood Lowe's to buy some deck-building materials, an item unexpectedly caught my eye. Amid issues of *Fine Woodworking* and *Creative Gardening* was a magazine entitled *The Happiness Formula: How to Find Joy & Live Your Best Life*. I had to buy it, even at the ridiculous price of $12.99. The magazine is a glossy ninety-five pages of articles, pro tips, charts, and graphs about the "science of happiness." In short, snappy prose, they tell us how "modern science" (by which they mean the branch of psychotherapy called positive psychology) teaches us what things to do and not do to be happy. Eat right. Avoid bad relationships. Ride bicycles more, like the happy Swedish people do. Practice yoga. Even a home improvement store is offering help on the happiness question.

And why not? After all, this is what it means to be an American. It's right there in our Declaration of Independence. The great American experiment was self-consciously rooted in the French Enlightenment view of humanity—that all humans are created equal, with inalienable rights. Among these rights a big three are stated explicitly—"Life, Liberty and," wait for it, "the pursuit of Happiness." I'm not being snarky. There are plenty of problems with the French Enlightenment and with American culture, but they're onto something here that is bigger than France or the United States. The desire for happiness is universally human and not wrong.

But humans, we have a problem. I don't mean the big issues that fill our newsfeeds and spark heated debates—racial tensions, social and economic inequity, definitions of sexuality, polarized political parties, even global pandemics. These are real issues, but they're not the human problem I'm talking about.

I'm talking about a wider, deeper, and older problem that can be boiled down to the question of *meaningful happiness*. Does any of what we do *really* matter? Does it have ultimate and lasting meaning? And will this meaningfulness make me happy? These are not just the musings of nineteen-year-olds in their first philosophy class but are questions that all humans eventually ask themselves. And it's not just a modern existential question. The Old Testament book of Ecclesiastes records the exact same wrestling by an ancient Near Eastern guy.

The fact that we all eventually ask that question shows there's something to it. So then we must ask, *How* do we live meaningful lives? How do we find and maintain true happiness? This is the question at the foundation of human experience. Without meaning, life is not worth living. Only humans die by suicide.[1] Even many who do not choose to end their own lives eventually feel like the philosophical superhero Deadpool, who remarks sardonically, "Life is an endless series of train wrecks with only brief, commercial-like breaks of happiness."[2]

○ ○ ○ ○

Saint Augustine, like countless thinkers before and after him, traced the essence of human meaningfulness to true happiness. When we talk about meaningfulness, we're talking about the universal human drive to be truly and lastingly happy. Book 10 of Augustine's massive tome *The City of God* begins this way: "It is the decided opinion of all who use their brains, that all men desire to be happy."[3] Happiness is what all humans want; people cannot *not* want happiness. This is what it means to have a brain. This is what it means to be human.

The Greeks had a word for this ultimate meaningfulness: *eudaimonia*, which we can translate as "soul happiness" or "flourishing." In his five-hundred-page scholarly work on the topic, *Happiness: A History*, Darrin McMahon discusses Herodotus, who wrote the first history of the West. Herodotus's grand story is set as a quest for happiness, which can be described with several Greek words—*makarios* (happy), *olbios* (prosperous), and *eutychia* (luck). But finally Herodotus uses the word *eudaimonia*—soul happiness, flourishing—to capture the subtleties of all these ideas.[4]

But even though the great Greeks have given us a word for true soul happiness, that doesn't mean it is easy to find it and keep it. Moreover, happiness is not only difficult to find and keep, but it's not even clear exactly what soul happiness is. Augustine continues his *City of God* discussion: "But who the happy ones are, or how they become so, are questions about which the weakness of human understanding stirs endless and angry controversies."[5]

In other words, everyone who has pondered the big questions of life agrees that meaningful happiness is the goal. What people vary wildly on is *what* this happiness looks like and *how* to obtain it. For some it is a religion of duty and sacrifice. For others it is freedom from any constraints or commands. For some, happiness is found in family, friends, and food, in being aware of the goodness and beauty of such things in the moment and in memory. For others achievement, honor, success, and wealth appear to be the way to capture the elusive happiness. But we'd all agree that even though the desire for happiness is universal, it's incredibly difficult to find and maintain. Humans, we have a problem.

○ ○ ○ ○

In his international bestseller *Sapiens*, Yuval Noah Harari traces human history over what he understands to be a two-and-a-half-million-year process of evolutionary biology. He's writing a large-scale history not just of human civilization but of the human species itself. *Homo sapiens*—that's us—are simply an "animal of no significance" that has ended up dominating over other genera of animals.[6]

According to Harari, in the unpredictable and uncontrollable process of evolution, *Homo sapiens* went through three revolutions that enabled us to outlast the others and to have a place in the earth's ecosystem that is so advanced that we can even write books about ourselves. Harari describes the three *Homo sapiens* revolutions as the Cognitive, the Agricultural, and the Scientific. We rule over the world (for the most part) because we alone among animals can believe in things that exist only in our imaginations—mental realities such as gods, money, nation-states, and rights.

After hundreds of interesting pages of broad-brush discussion, Harari brings his discussion down to two specific points. One is his ponderings about the future of our species in light of genetic engineering and cybernetic enhancements. The other is the question of happiness. His penultimate chapter is entitled "And They Lived Happily Ever After." Harari states the problematic question well:

> The last 500 years have witnessed a breathtaking series of revolutions. The earth has been united into a single ecological and historical sphere. The economy has grown exponentially, and humankind today enjoys the kind of wealth that used to be the stuff of fairy tales. Science and the Industrial Revolution have given humankind superhuman powers and practically limitless energy. The social order has been completely transformed, as have politics, daily life and human psychology.

But are we happier? Did the wealth humankind accumulated over the last five centuries translate into a new-found contentment? . . . [Has the] Cognitive Revolution made the world a better place to live in? Was the late Neil Armstrong, whose footprint remains intact on the windless moon, happier than the nameless hunter-gatherer who 30,000 years ago left her handprint on a wall in Chauvet Cave?[7]

Are we happier? This is the question we can't avoid, nor should we. Harari's short answer is no, in fact, we don't seem to be happier today, though he notes this is a very difficult thing to assess historically. We simply don't know whether a medieval peasant was happy. We can't just project our own life experiences and expectations onto someone else's and assume we can evaluate what they thought of their lives. By *our* culturally conditioned standards we can't imagine a peasant being happy, but that's making a big assumption. Discerning happiness depends on how we define it. If happiness is measured by material metrics such as diet, wealth, and longevity, as if these guarantee happiness, then modern humans must be happier than our predecessors. But it is not apparently the case that moderns are happier.

The real issue, Harari notes, is our tendency today to define happiness as a kind of emotional mathematics: we are happy if the sum of our more pleasant moments is more than the sum of our unpleasant ones. The average person today has been enculturated to think this way, defining happiness in terms of mere emotions. Instead, as Harari rightly points out, true "happiness consists in seeing one's life in its entirety as meaningful and worthwhile."[8]

There it is. Happiness and meaningfulness entail each other. Whether one interprets caring for a crying infant in the middle of the night as "lovingly nurturing a new life" or as "being a slave to a baby dictator" depends on whether we evaluate our actions as meaningful. And if what we do is meaningful then we can find soul happiness / *eudaimonia* even in the midst of hardship.[9]

○ ○ ○ ○

In another recent bestseller, *All Things Shining*, the philosophers Hubert Dreyfus and Sean Dorrance Kelly open with these striking lines: "The world doesn't matter to us the way it used to. The intense and meaningful lives of Homer's Greeks, and the grand hierarchy of meaning that structured Dante's medieval Christian world, both stand in stark contrast to our secular age. The world used to be, in its various forms, a world of sacred, shining things. The shining things now seem far away. This book is intended to bring them close once more."[10]

There it is again: "intense and *meaningful* lives" and "the grand hierarchy of *meaning*"—or as they describe it memorably, "shining." They are talking about happiness. Dreyfus and Kelly's subtitle is important: *Reading the Western Classics to Find Meaning in a Secular Age*. We are now in a secular age, the authors note, an age when neither the polytheism of the ancient Greeks nor the monotheism of the Christian world holds sway. And the result, Dreyfus and Kelly readily admit, is that it is very hard to find meaning, to figure out how to live a meaningful life.

Dreyfus and Kelly are more pointed and philosophical than Harari in their assessment of happiness: We modern humans are in an existential crisis, they argue. Nihilism—the understanding that nothing really matters—is the air we breathe in the modern secular age. And this is bad news for humanity.

Humans today, especially in the West, live in a psychological space where the old structures, both pagan and Christian, have broken down and been replaced with a scientific understanding of the world. This enables us to send a probe to Saturn but find it difficult to live meaningful lives. While most people walking around aren't *committed* nihilists—this is more often the

190

felt experience of artists and philosophers—they struggle to find a comprehensive worldview that makes life meaningful. It is hard to be happy. If it weren't, we wouldn't have 577,000 mental health professionals, 15 million people suffering from depression, and a $10 billion industry in bibliotherapy (self-help books). This is just in the United States alone.[11]

○ ○ ○ ○

Harari, Dreyfus, and Kelly are all philosophers trying to help us understand life. Whether they realize it or not, they are standing on the shoulders of the giants of a tradition of human-helping that goes back as far as human civilization itself.

It turns out that the question of meaningful happiness and how to find it is not new. It is not just a function of modern humanity's experience. It is as old as thinking humanity itself. Remember Augustine's comment about the drive for happiness? He wrote that in the early 400s AD. By that time, the philosophical discussion about happiness and meaning was at least seven hundred to eight hundred years old in the Western tradition and even older in the ancient Near East and Far East. In the Greek and Roman tradition, thinkers we've met already, like Socrates, Plato, Aristotle, Epictetus, and Seneca, all pondered the great questions of happiness and offered practical, real-life wisdom on how to live well. The nineteen-year-old students pondering this in their philosophy class are onto something important and deeply human. They're thinking about the right question. The "sapiens" part of our *Homo sapiens* designation refers to "wisdom" (Latin, *sapientia*). What distinguishes our version of creatureliness is our thinkingness, our insatiable pursuit of understanding, of meaningfulness.

○ ○ ○ ○

Throughout this book we've met several ancient philosophers, and we've seen that they were thoughtful, sophisticated thinkers who cared about real, practical life. They developed schools of philosophy and made evangelistic disciples not so they could get cushy professorial jobs (well, at least not the sincere ones) but so that they could help themselves and other people learn how to live well. So all their explorations about physics, metaphysics, ethics, politics, emotions, and relationships funnel down to this greatest of human questions: How do we find meaningful happiness? Everything else the ancient philosophers talked about always had this human flourishing goal as the ultimate purpose.

We don't need to rehearse what Plato, Aristotle, Epicurus, and Seneca said about emotions and relationships. We do need to close the loop on our reflections by recognizing how this is all connected to meaningful happiness.

The reason these thinkers thought so much about emotions, the importance of friendships, the role of the government in relationship to the individual, and how to handle anxiety is because (1) they knew that the drive for flourishing was central and universal to human experience, and (2) they knew that learning to order our emotions and relationships is crucial to our meaningful happiness.

For the Greek and Roman tradition—the notable exception being the hedonists—the flourishing and happy life does not happen accidentally. It must be sought after. And the means of pursuit is the life of discipleship to a philosophy, a way of seeing and being in the world that is pursued and practiced. First become aware of yourself; then turn away from foolish and non-life-giving habits and thoughts (in biblical language, "repent"); and then, over time, learn new ways of living through failures and successes in practice.

There were differences, certainly, between what Aristotle, Epicurus, and Marcus Aurelius said about all kinds of issues. They didn't agree, for example, on what role physical pleasures played in true happiness. And Aurelius, following good Stoic practice, meditated each morning on all the bad things that might happen to him. There's no indication this habit would be recommended by Aristotle. These differences in philosophy and practice are inevitable because each of their teachings was tied to their own understanding of the world that affected how they practiced life. Also, each person's life experience is different. As the old saying goes, "All theology is autobiography"—so too with the ancient philosophers. Why we are inclined to think and practice life in certain ways is always embedded in our own particular experiences.

So they disagreed on lots of habits and beliefs, but they all shared this central idea: We long for flourishing, and the only way to find it is through living intentionally and thoughtfully in particular ways. Neither virtue nor its eventual fruit, happiness, comes to us accidentally.

○ ○ ○ ○

Even though today's philosophers rarely traffic in the great question of happiness like their predecessors did, this doesn't mean we've stopped having happiness-purveyors. We have lots of them. Even if most professional philosophers have abdicated this role, humans, like water obeying gravity, will always find gurus to guide us to happiness.

Today we have countless happiness gurus of all sorts, shapes, and sizes. Most are sincere and helpful; some are manipulative and malignant. A lot of them provide some help. Some provide a lot of help. And some of them provide good help that is misapplied by bad people. The story goes that while in prison for car theft, Charles Manson read and became obsessed with Dale Carnegie's famous self-help book *How to Win Friends and Influence People*. Just over ten years later, having founded a California cult centered on himself, he influenced his "family" to commit atrocious murders.[12] No one is happy with Manson's particular application, but all agree that Carnegie is an example of a guru of meaningful happiness.

193

I wrote much of the last half of this book in the beautiful new, modern, angular glass-and-steel Northeast Regional Library that's within walking distance of my house. Even in the modest holdings of this library are several rows of books designed to help people figure out their lives and how to be happy. Titles include *Lagom: The Swedish Art of Balanced Living*, *You Are the Placebo*, *10% Happier*, *Stick with It*, *The Happiness Equation*, and *The Secret* (which obviously must not be so any longer). These are just a few random titles that I see as I walk by those shelves during my intralibrary circumnavigation break. Let's take a brief walk through a couple of the myriad of happinesses on offer today.

○ ○ ○ ○

A good place to start is with Alain de Botton and his School of Life. I first encountered de Botton when devouring his beautiful and fascinating book *Art as Therapy*. This handsome volume (you should spend a little more and get the hardback) is full of images of art and architecture. This remarkable book resists classification. At first you may think it is just a pretty art-history coffee-table book, but soon you realize much more is going on as it moves quickly and digs deeply across a wide range of psychological, personal, and social issues. You'll be forced to think profoundly, and not just about lofty ideas. You'll soon be pondering your feelings of anxiety, envy, and what it means to love. I've gone on to read several other books by de Botton, who really is a twenty-first-century version of an ancient philosopher. Today this comes complete with all that modernization means—many published bestsellers, TED talks, YouTube lectures, and even a BBC Channel 4 series on philosophy.

What ties *Art as Therapy* together is the conviction that our intentional engaging of visual art can help us lead better lives. For de Botton (and his coauthor, John Armstrong) this means accessing "better versions of ourselves."[13] The great function of visual art, they argue, is to use it as a tool for our therapy. This therapy is our growth to becoming better versions of ourselves through being guided, exhorted, consoled, and enabled by what art offers.[14] Visual art, when interpreted soul-therapeutically, helps us with our psychological frailties and needs. Art channels to us the importance of remembering, hope, sorrow, self-understanding, growth, and appreciation. Art helps us with our most intimate and ordinary dilemmas.

De Botton and Armstrong are using art and architecture to consciously address the great human questions of happiness and meaning. Their book is only one part of a larger project they are engaged in called the School of Life. The School of Life is, according to its website, "a global organisation dedicated to developing emotional intelligence" through applying psychology, philosophy, and culture to everyday life.[15] This philosophy of emotional intelligence is worked out through the production of books like *Art as Therapy* and also through a wide range of human development workshops conducted by experts all over the world, centered in these city-based schools. Sounds a lot like ancient Greek philosophy.

One such workshop is entitled "Finding Meaning without Religion." Quite similar to Dreyfus and Kelly's *All Things Shining*, this workshop starts with the recognition that modern people (at least in the West) have the freedom to choose religion or not. No single religion or philosophy dominates our culture now, unlike before. This has its downside, the seminar notes, because we are conscious of a "God-shaped hole"—a sense of a higher purpose—that we aren't sure what to do about with no authoritative answer.[16]

De Botton has written a whole book along these lines, with the intriguing title *Religion for Atheists*. He is a committed atheist and makes this clear on page 1. He doesn't believe in miracles or "tales of burning shrubbery." But unlike most intellectual atheists, de Botton is not content to focus only on critiquing religions for their problems and irrationalities. Quite the opposite, he is interested in helping his fellow committed atheists rediscover that organized religions contain human thoughts and practices that can be useful, interesting, and even consoling. According to de Botton, even though the doctrine of the Christian Trinity or the Buddhist Eightfold Path can leave one cold, there are many ways in which religions help humans live morally, develop community, and inspire us to appreciate beauty—to live the Good Life. Atheists have a lot to learn from religions, he says.

De Botton states that our predecessors invented religions to serve two central needs: (1) the need to live together in communities in harmony even though we are deeply selfish and at times violent, and (2) the need to cope with fear, pain, difficulties, and ultimately death. Even though de Botton rejects the truthfulness of any religious claim, he notes that these two issues still exist in our secular society and that we've not done a particularly good job of developing skills to deal with them. Once we get free from the compulsion to worship gods or to denigrate them, then "we are free to discover religions as repositories of a myriad of ingenious concepts with which we can try to assuage a few of the most persistent and unattended ills of secular life."[17] These "ingenious concepts" include the notions of community, kindness, education, institutions, art, and architecture.

De Botton is a clear and fascinating writer. His insights are noteworthy, stimulating, and memorable. This includes lots of quirky but profound graphics, such as the chart comparing Pringles sales to the number of poetry books sold in a given year. *Religion for Atheists*, *Art as Therapy*, and the School of Life all promise the way to a meaningful life. De Botton's philosophy of life is far more sophisticated and helpful than slapping a "Coexist" bumper sticker on one's car, whether aggressively or peacefully. From a Christian perspective, the ultimate question of *what is true* is still unavoidable. Nonetheless, de Botton exemplifies thoughtful humanity wrestling with the universal questions of how to find and live meaningfully happy lives.

○ ○ ○ ○

Top-ten movie lists are dangerous things to offer—so I won't—but I will say that for me, somewhere in that enumeration is one you probably haven't heard of: *Hector and the Search for Happiness*. Rotten Tomatoes and other rating systems generally rank it pretty low, so you'll have to decide for yourself, but I love it. It's a 2014 movie starring Simon Pegg, based on a French novel of the same name by François Lelord.

Hector is an English psychiatrist who lives a very safe and organized life but who increasingly realizes he is not happy. He also realizes he's not really helping his clients become any happier. So, uncharacteristically, he sets out on a quest to discover happiness. His journey takes him to China, where he experiences both the high life in an exclusive nightclub and the deep inward journey with Himalayan monks. He visits an old friend in Africa, eventually being ambushed and left to suffer in a rat-infested prison. Finally, he goes to California to try to reconnect with the college lover that he let get away. In all of these situations he both suffers and finds moments of joy. But deep and lasting happiness remains elusive, even while his relationship with his longtime girlfriend in London is deteriorating.

Finally, while in Los Angeles, Hector meets a professor who lectures on happiness and is doing brain-scan research on emotions. Professor Coreman asks the haunting question, "How many of us can recall a moment when we experienced happiness as a state of being, that single moment of untarnished joy, that moment when everything in our world, inside and out, was alright?" It's elusive, isn't it? His conclusion is that "we should not concern ourselves so much with the pursuit of happiness, but with the happiness of pursuit."[18]

Spoiler alert: Stop reading now if you don't want to hear about the climactic moment. The movie ends with Hector in the neurologist's booth experiencing a block—he can't feel anything. He is directed to think about times he was happy, sad, and scared. He can recall memories, but he can't connect to his emotions. And then, finally, he breaks, and the scans explode with color and activity. He finally discovers that happiness is found not just in one positive emotion but in embracing all of his emotions and experiences. It's a very powerful scene that never fails to make me cry.

Along the journey before this point, Hector scribbles his reflections on happiness in his notebook. The result is a list of eighteen insights about happiness. It is this potentially pedantic technique that has made some readers of the novel feel it is more of a "maudlin self-help guide" than a story.[19] That may be more true of the novel than it is for the movie. Nonetheless, these eighteen tips provide a guide for human happiness, very much like the Stoics and other ancient philosophers provided.

Here are some of them:

- Making comparisons can spoil your happiness.
- Avoiding unhappiness is not the road to happiness.
- Happiness is answering your calling.
- Happiness is being loved for who you are.
- Happiness is knowing how to celebrate.
- Nostalgia is not what it used to be.

Once again we find ourselves on a quest for happiness. Life is complex and difficult. We instinctively know there is an elusive happiness out there—we've tasted it more than once. How do we find it? Are pithy aphorisms the solution?

○ ○ ○ ○

Anyone who has ever had a class on world religions or gotten into debates online about the exclusiveness of various faiths has probably eventually run into the "blind men and the elephant" illustration. The story goes something like this: There are several blind men walking together, and they encounter an elephant. Because they are blind and each only experiences part of the elephant, they all have different interpretations. Feeling the tusk, one says it is a spear. Encountering the trunk leads one to believe it is a snake. A rope or tree are the natural interpretations for those feeling the tail or legs. Who is right? Well, none of them and each of them. Each blind man—like each religion—only sees a part of the truth. And from the limited part they see, they make a reasonable interpretation, so the story goes.

So too with the seemingly infinite number of philosophies of happiness. Just in the ancient world alone, people disagreed significantly about how to find flourishing. Do we need to detach ourselves from emotions, or is the key ecstatic temple-based experiences? When we follow human thought down to today, the differing philosophies of life-happiness are myriad and overwhelming. Is it a keto diet, CrossFit, entrenching into "Make America Great Again" values, finding inner peace through hot yoga, daily journaling, making sure you "pay it forward" every day, etc., etc., etc.? There are simply too many choices, like the menu at the Cheesecake Factory. It can feel paralyzing.

Moreover—and partially a result of this overwhelming feeling—few of today's philosophies are even attempting to give us something comprehensive. Most philosophies of happiness on tap are very particular in their focus and make no metaphysical claims to explain all of reality. Peloton's quite pricey but apparently effective internet-connected bike exercise

Figure 14
Elephant and blind men

program provides an "immersive cardio experience," but it doesn't promise to help you figure out mothers-in-law or the fear of death. This limitedness is typical.

Alain de Botton's School of Life is the most comprehensive nonreligious philosophy of happiness I have found today. It is modeled, at least in part, on the ancient philosophical schools, and this is no accident. Most of the gurus that people look to today offer only a limited kind of happiness—happiness in the realm of parenting, or of business sales, or in marriage, or in physical exercise. De Botton's School of Life is the closest thing to a whole-life philosophy of happiness, but it is still limited.

So who is right? Are we all just blind philosophers encountering a part of the elephant of life with no hope of a comprehensive philosophy of happiness?

Christianity's Whole, Meaningful, and Flourishing Life

Back at the beginning of our journey exploring Jesus as the Great Philosopher, we met one of his earliest followers, Justin the Philosopher-turned-Martyr. Justin represents the primal understanding of Christianity as a philosophy. Indeed, Christianity is the truest philosophy of the world because it is based on the person of Jesus, the incarnated Son of God.

This conviction means that, while there may be good ideas and practices that can be gleaned from other philosophies and religions, they are only partial. In comparison with the Christian philosophy, all other views on relationships, emotions, and happiness are fractional and incomplete (and sometimes just flat wrong). Or to think of it constructively, because Jesus is the actual Logos—the organizing principle of the world, the agent of creation, the being that holds the whole universe together—this means that *his* philosophy alone is whole, complete, and truly true. How's that for a physic behind a metaphysic that gives us an ethic and politic?

So let's intersect this powerful truth with the famous blind men and the elephant story. Each of these blind philosophers understands to the best of their ability. But Christianity makes

Figure 15
Elephant, blind men, and Jesus

a claim that is inherently transcendent—Jesus is not just another wise man or insightful sage. He stands above, around, and outside of this whole philosophical elephantine situation. He alone sees the whole and sees correctly and therefore alone can proclaim truly and fully, "It's an elephant!"

This image helpfully depicts the reality of Jesus the Great Philosopher and Christianity as the true philosophy of the world. However, this otherwise good analogy breaks down in one important way. Namely, the blind philosophers in this story are each *entirely* wrong regarding the actual elephant, thinking the tail is a rope, the leg a tree trunk, and so on. While this analogy works for the point of the illustration—that every religion sees imperfectly—it doesn't quite work for what I'm trying to say. That is, Jesus's all-seeing perspective does not necessarily mean that all the insights of other religions and philosophies are completely wrong. None of them have the complete perspective that Christianity does, but this does not mean *everything* they say is entirely mistaken. It only means every other philosophical view is partial.

Hence, as we have seen throughout this book, there is insight to be gained from what the philosophers said about all sorts of topics. We needn't cut ourselves completely off from their wisdom. Rather, we can gather lumber from whatever trees are available as we build the Christ-shaped temple of our lives, with Holy Scripture as the building inspector. As Justin himself said, "Whatever things were rightly said among all men, are the property of us Christians. . . . For all the writers [ancient philosophers and poets] were able to see realities darkly through the sowing of the implanted word that was in them. For the seed and imitation that is imparted according to capacity is one thing, and quite another is the thing itself, of which there is the participation and imitation according to the grace which is from Him."[1]

That last part gets a bit complex, but the point is straightforward—any wisdom in the world is from God, who created all, but we Christians have the grace that enables complete understanding. This includes the grandest human philosophical question: What does it mean to live a whole, meaningful, and flourishing life? What is the wisdom we need for the Good Life?

○ ○ ○ ○

The monk Elder Zosima is the moral center of Fyodor Dosto-evsky's sweeping novel *The Brothers Karamazov*. While discussing his impending death with a noble lady, she remarks that Zosima looks so happy, despite his deteriorating health. He responds, "If I seem happy to you there is nothing you could ever say that would please me so much. For men are made for happiness. And anyone who is completely happy has a right to say to himself, 'I am doing God's will on earth.' All the righteous, all the saints, all the holy martyrs are happy."[2]

This sounds odd. If we conducted another "Word on the Street" interview and asked people what comes to mind for the word "happy," I doubt many people, if anyone, would say, "The righteous, the saints, the holy martyrs"—no matter how many people we interviewed. And if we asked it in the converse way—How would you describe the righteous, saints, and holy martyrs?—I bet the responses would include adjectives like "uptight, anxious, and angry," not "happy." "Happiness" and "Christianity" aren't related in our minds. They're not even cousins.

The same could be said for "Christianity" and "philosophy." In modern usage, these words are two different worlds, as intimately related as spark plugs and cheese. But in reality, Elder Zosima's confident comment, the philosophical tradition of seeking happiness, and the Christian faith are all deeply interwoven. They are strands of one tapestry.

Saint Augustine said it this way: "No one has any right to philosophize except with a view to happiness."[3] Augustine understands his Christian faith to be about philosophy and about happiness. This is because philosophy, understood correctly—whether it is from Moses, Aristotle, de Botton, or Jesus—is about meaningful happiness. And if Christianity is true and significant, then it too will address this greatest of human questions.

The Polish theologian Darius Karłowicz sums it up this way: "The task of all philosophy, including Christian philosophy, is the therapy of souls who have been led astray by the demands of the passions and false pictures of happiness."[4] Christianity is engaged in the great work of reshaping humanity into the image of Christ (Rom. 8:29; 2 Cor. 3:18). This is a soul therapy that promises to bring humanity back into a life of meaningfulness. Jesus sums up his own purpose as coming into the world "that they may have life, and have it to the full" (John 10:10).

Key to this soul therapy is challenging misunderstandings about happiness that humanity has imbibed. It means guiding people to discover ways of inhabiting the world that will lead to meaningful happiness—all based on the revelation of God in Jesus Christ. Christianity is a philosophy of happiness.

○○○○

Christianity is a philosophy of happiness because it is based on the Bible, and the Bible is constantly addressing these same grand questions of meaning and happiness.[5] As one small window into this, we can consider the first poem of the great collection of Israel's songs and prayers, what is called the Psalter. Psalm 1 addresses the question of meaningful happiness right out of the chute, centering happiness in a life orientation toward God:

> [Happy/Flourishing] is the one
>> who does not walk in step with the wicked
> or stand in the way that sinners take
>> or sit in the company of mockers,
> but whose delight is in the law of the LORD,
>> and who meditates on his law day and night.
> That person is like a tree planted by streams of water,
>> which yields its fruit in season
> and whose leaf does not wither—
>> whatever they do prospers.
>
> Not so the wicked!
>> They are like chaff
>> that the wind blows away.
> Therefore the wicked will not stand in the judgment,
>> nor sinners in the assembly of the righteous.
>
> For the LORD watches over the way of the righteous,
>> but the way of the wicked leads to destruction.

So right here in the first song that all Hebrew children and adults sing and all Christian monks and nuns chant repeatedly throughout the week and year is the issue of true happiness. The very first topic in this 150-song book that explores the full gamut of human emotions and experiences is the question of flourishing. The Bible cares about the Good Life.

This tone-setting psalm is intentionally mirrored right at the beginning of Jesus's ministry too. Jesus's famous Sermon on the Mount starts with his Beatitudes, his authoritative declarations about what true happiness (*beatus*) is. Jesus's celebrated instructions start with exactly the same word that Psalm 1 does—"Happy/Flourishing."[6]

> Happy/Flourishing are the poor in spirit, for the kingdom of heaven is theirs.
> Happy/Flourishing are those who mourn, for they will be comforted.
> Happy/Flourishing are the meek, for they will inherit the earth. (Matt. 5:3–5, my translation)

In the Beatitudes, Jesus gives nine statements about what true happiness or the Good Life looks like now and in the age to come. In fact, in some early biblical manuscripts the *whole* Sermon on the Mount (Matt. 5–7) was titled "Concerning Happiness," because it was clear to Matthew's readers that this is what Jesus was offering. Jesus is a philosopher of happiness.

I think we can confidently say—even though it sounds odd today and could be misunderstood—that at the very core of the Bible's message is the idea of true happiness and flourishing. "Shalom" is how the Old Testament describes it. "Flourishing" or "entering the kingdom" or "being glorified" or "entering life" is how the New Testament talks. It's all wrapped up together, no matter which words or metaphors we use. The Bible is a book about true happiness.

oooo

Does this sound odd? This may be because you've been taught that longing for happiness is a bad thing. But God himself is fully happy, and as creatures who are made in his image, we long for the same. And we had it once. In the prefall garden of Eden, Adam and Eve knew God and walked with God. And they were happy. It was a false promise of *more* flourishing that led to humanity's broken relationship with God and all its subsequent pain, suffering, and death. The serpent's offering of forbidden fruit was a hook for more happiness. Satan rightly appealed to the first humans' desire for abundant life as seen in the form of a tree. Tragically and ironically, it was this trusting of the wrong authority (Satan rather than God) that resulted in humanity's prohibition from being able to eat of the tree of eternal life (Gen. 3:22–24)—the very thing we all long for.[7] The problem was not the *desire for happiness* but rather the wrong way in which they pursued it.

That is a crucially important distinction. This distinction begins to address a potential big objection to what I've just been saying. Someone may fairly ask, "What about self-denial? What about Jesus's call to take up our cross and follow him?" How in the world could I be saying that the Bible cares about happiness in light of this? Isn't all this talk about happiness and flourishing just another version of the plastic-smiled and deceptive health-and-wealth gospel?

Those are fair and understandable questions. I would respond by noting that the desire for happiness is not inherently wrong. The Bible nowhere condemns the desire. Quite the opposite—the desire for happiness is assumed. But it is easy to throw the proverbial baby out with the bathwater when we see how easily and thoroughly the desire for happiness gets corrupted. We've all heard people appeal to their own happiness as the basis for abandoning one's family and running off with the secretary. And we've heard a hundred other misappropriations.

But the problem here, once again, is not the desire for happiness but the means by which it is pursued.

○ ○ ○ ○

For countless Christians in contemporary America, speaking of "desire" and "God" in the same sentence will make us think of the great preacher John Piper. I first read his hugely influential book *Desiring God* shortly after it came out, when I was a fresh college-aged believer. It was transformative for me, as it has been for thousands of others. The book you're holding in your hands is not one that I think Piper would ever write for many reasons, but I believe our projects have a deep resonance and harmony. They are written in the same key—the key of longing and desire for true happiness and flourishing. I don't imagine Piper loves Pink Floyd as much as I do, but I think he would affirm the universal sentiment of human longing and loss expressed in their classic song "Comfortably Numb." David Gilmour refers to his childhood as a time when he caught a fleeting glimpse of happiness, but then it eluded him. Now, "The child is grown / The dream is gone."

Piper's original *Desiring God* subtitle—*Meditations of a Christian Hedonist*—raised eyebrows in its day. I'm not a big fan of this subtitle because of the importance difference between hedonism and philosophy. But I appreciate what he's getting at. Piper's point is that not only is it okay to have desires for happiness, but happiness is also necessary for a proper relationship with God. If we approach God with duty or obligation as a primary motivation, not love and desire, then we don't have a true relationship—we have mere religion.

Early on in his book, Piper gives a lengthy quote from the always-insightful C. S. Lewis that is worth repeating here: "If there lurks in most modern minds the notion that to desire our own good and earnestly to hope for the enjoyment of it is a bad thing, I submit that this notion has crept in from Kant and the Stoics and is no part of the Christian faith. Indeed, if we consider the unblushing promises of reward in the Gospels, it would seem that Our Lord finds our desires [for happiness] not too strong, but too weak." This is from Lewis's beautiful sermon "The Weight of Glory." He goes on to famously say, "We are half-hearted creatures, fooling about with drink and sex and ambition when infinite joy is offered to us, like an ignorant child who wants to go on making mud pies in a slum because he cannot imagine what is meant by the offer of a holiday at the sea."[8]

That reference to Kant is especially important and deeply relevant to the vision I'm casting here for Christianity as the true philosophy of happiness. Here specifically, Lewis, and by proxy Piper, is tapping into one of the most disastrous ideas of Kant, the notion that for an action to be virtuous and good, the agent/actor must *not* get any personal benefit from it. This benefit especially includes one's own flourishing and happiness. Kant's idea of a good action is called "altruism."

Altruism has become so deeply embedded in modern ethics that most Christians do not realize how thoroughly unbiblical it is. And this is what Lewis and Piper are getting at. Altruism is indeed death to biblical (and ancient philosophical) ethics. Lewis's and Piper's point, and mine as well, is that it is precisely the desire for happiness that drives *all* that we do. And that's okay. It is how God made us and exactly how God motivates us. It is the "staggering rewards" that Jesus continually promises us that are not condemned but commended. (I'm not sure Lewis is entirely fair to throw the Stoics under the bus here, but Kant definitely needs a curbside push on this matter.)

The biblical emphasis on rewards from God as motivation means that the ideas we hear from Jesus about "self-sacrifice" and "cross-bearing" must not be misconstrued. These cross-bearing commands do not mean denial of our own desires for happiness, as if somehow a duty-only approach is a virtue. Altruistic self-denial is neither a virtue nor what Jesus is saying.

The call to lay down narcissistic self-absorption and to serve others even at a cost to our conveniences, finances, and luxuries is real (Phil. 2:1–11). But this is never an appeal to abstract duty; it is instead an invitation to *true* happiness. "It is more blessed [the same word as in the Beatitudes] to give than to receive" (Acts 20:35) is not a Kantian statement of duty but an invitation to wisdom, to reorienting our hearts toward what will *truly* bring the fountain of flourishing to our dry souls. The call on our lives is not a denial of desire but a reordering of our loves for the greatest good for us, others, and God's honor. As Lewis's devil Screwtape explains to his tempter in training, when the Enemy (God) instructs humans to lose themselves, "He only means abandoning the clamour of self-will; once they have done that, He really gives them back all their personality."[9] Self-denial is the means to soul-fullness.

This was even Jesus's own motivation. Jesus, the perfect human, had real desires and motives that were not merely obedient duty. He was motivated by desire. Why in the world would this sinless, beautiful, caring God-man be willing to endure mocking, misrepresentation, physical privation, and ultimately torture and death? What would make you willing to do so? Kantian duty?

No. We're told exactly why—*for the joy that he would gain and enter into as a result!* Hebrews 12:2 sums it up with the invitation for us to look to Jesus's own example here, to "fix our eyes" on him as the model and pioneer of what it means to relate to God rightly. It was "for the joy set before him [that] he endured the cross, scorning its shame, and sat down at the right hand of the throne of God." Jesus was motivated by his own future happiness.

And now we can come full circle to our discussion of the genius of ancient philosophy. Kant's very different approach to ethics is precisely what happened to modern philosophy to make it only "screw you up for the rest of your life," as Steve Martin quipped. Modern philosophy is abstract, depersonalized, and doesn't help us learn to live well. But ancient philosophy did. And so does biblical Christianity.

The ancient Christian philosophy offers a remarkably sophisticated understanding of what it means to pursue and find true happiness in this broken and disappointing world. The fact that we have stopped thinking that this is what Holy Scripture is offering is not a function of the Bible's actual teaching but of the undue influence of this whole approach to life that modern philosophy has promoted. Thanks, Kant.

○○○○

So what does this sophisticated Christian philosophy of a whole, meaningful, and flourishing life look like? As we have seen with the topic of emotions and relationships, Christianity does not offer simplistic, bumper-sticker platitudes. Instead, when we dial in on the question of flourishing in Holy Scripture, we find a robust and nuanced answer.

The Old Testament begins with a tragic two-step story of paradise made and paradise lost. Within only the first three chapters of the great Genesis creation story we see humans move from the experience of flourishing in the presence of God to shame, regret, fear, loss, and death. What follows is a story of increasing degradation, suffering, conflict, homicide, grief, humanity-massacring floods, sodomy, deceit, and rape.

Where is flourishing in all of this? It is found in glimpses when people turn to God, lifting their eyes from earth to heaven. People like Noah, Abraham, Sarah, Isaac, Rebekah, Leah, Jacob, and Rachel taste bits of true happiness in hors d'oeuvres–sized moments of faith and obedience. They briefly reflect what it means to be fully human and happy, like an image in a shattered mirror.

But this imperfect experience of flourishing in the biblical stories does not belie the emphasis that Scripture puts on true happiness. Quite the contrary, the biblical story of brokenness and sin explains why humans universally long for shalom, for a whole and meaningful life. As a result, the arc of the whole story of Israel is one of hope—certain hope for a coming age when God will return, bring justice, and establish peace throughout his marred creation and in his distorted creatures. This is the hope of the coming kingdom of God, especially highlighted in the Old Testament prophets, and most especially in Isaiah.

The book of Psalms is the divinely given songbook and therapeutic manual during this time of waiting. The Psalms embrace the reality of brokenness, longing, disappointment, injustice, and death. Yet, as we noted above, the very first word of the Psalter casts a vision for the possibility of happiness and flourishing—now and yet more to come.

This is remarkably sophisticated. The Old Testament is not an idealized mythology of easy happiness. It is not a philosophy that proclaims all suffering to be inconsequential or unreal. Neither is it a hopeless story of sin and destruction or postmodern literary antiheroes. *No, the story of Israel from creation through the prophets casts a vision of the possibility of deep flourishing even in the midst of inevitable loss and suffering.*

This vision serves as the essential backstory and scenery of the message that the New Testament proclaims. Jesus has now arrived to reverse the paradise lost! The promised shalomifying reign of God is finally here because the divine Son-King has returned home. This means the creation itself will begin to undergo a reversal, a reality that was first typified by physical phenomena at Jesus's death and resurrection, the regreening of the gray world. The events like darkness at noon, the temple curtain being torn in two, and the raising of dead people from their graves (Matt. 27:45–54) are symbols of a new creation coming. This also means that humans who share in the Son's Spirit-filled resurrection life will begin to experience a transformation away from cursedness to flourishing. The great ancient theologian Irenaeus famously described it this way: our Lord Jesus Christ "through His transcendent love became what we are that He might bring us to be even what He is Himself."[10]

Jesus not only brings into being this new age of flourishing in the midst of suffering but he also models for all humanity what this can look like. Jesus was a man of joy and love and peace. Whatever medievally inspired or puritanically stern images we might have of Jesus are simply not how the Gospels portray this man, who was accused of being a drunkard and friend of sinners. He was a happy and flourishing man. But he also suffered greatly. He experienced physical pain and emotional disappointment and frustration. He died not of natural causes but of the most unnatural—torture and suffocation at the hands of his enemies. He told his followers to expect the same. Yet he also constantly invites his disciples to be happy and to rejoice. In fact, in the very same breath, at the climactic conclusion to his nine-point discourse on happiness, he proclaims that true happiness can be found when you are "persecuted because of righteousness" and when people "insult you, persecute you and falsely say all kinds of evil against you" because of your association with Jesus (Matt. 5:10–11).

So, as with the Old Testament, the New Testament offers a nuanced and sophisticated—even paradoxical—philosophy of human flourishing or the Good Life. Jesus and his followers do not deny the reality of suffering. Neither do they encourage a closed-hearted "stiff upper lip" mentality. Rather, a whole, meaningful, and flourishing life is possible in the midst of brokenness and even unjust suffering.

There is a mystery and paradox here that is beyond human comprehension, but somehow suffering can even produce a greater and truer happiness. It's easy to fall off the knife-edge of this paradoxical truth on either side—seeking suffering masochistically or denying the divine good in difficulties. But Job and Jesus and countless other trusters in God have testified that trials, difficulties, and suffering have somehow brought about greater and deeper joy. The stars are brightest from inside the well. We may speculate that this has to do with a reorienting of our priorities and a refining of our desires for what is Good. But ultimately we must be content to embrace this truth without fully understanding it.

○ ○ ○ ○

How is this happiness-while-suffering paradox possible? The Christian philosophy's answer can be boiled down to one word: hope.

Hope is a funny thing. On the one hand, it is one of the three greatest abiding realities, according to 1 Corinthians 13:13: "And now these three remain: faith, hope and love." Forward-looking hope, as prominent New Testament scholar Richard Bauckham and theologian Trevor Hart have noted, is core to what it means to be a Christian: "To be a Christian, a person of faith, we might suggest is precisely to live as a person for whom God's future shapes the present."[11] To hope is to have faith.

Yet on the other hand, Christian hope has often been a particular point of derision from Christianity's opponents. From ancient times until today, Christianity's critics have often pointed to Christians' hope for a heavenly future as obscurantism and naive escapism. Unfortunately, even some within the Christian tradition have misstepped in this way.

We see the centrality of hope as a recurrent refrain throughout Scripture. Listen to how the apostle Paul describes hope's power and effects in the letter to the Romans:

> We also glory in our sufferings. . . . And hope does not put us to shame, because God's love has been poured out into our hearts through the Holy Spirit, who has been given to us. (5:3, 5)

For in this hope we were saved. But hope that is seen is no hope at all. Who hopes for what they already have? But if we hope for what we do not yet have, we wait for it patiently. (8:24–25)

Or consider the way the Psalms contrast two possible ways for us to live—as hoping in the people and things of this world versus hoping in God. Hope is another synonym for waiting and trusting in the Lord:

> But the face of the LORD is against those who do evil,
>   to blot out their name from the earth.
>
> The righteous cry out, and the LORD hears them;
>   he delivers them from all their troubles.
> The LORD is close to the brokenhearted
>   and saves those who are crushed in spirit.
>
> The righteous person may have many troubles,
>   but the LORD delivers him from them all;
> he protects all his bones,
>   not one of them will be broken.
>
> Evil will slay the wicked;
>   the foes of the righteous will be condemned.
>   (Ps. 34:16–21)

So in the Bible hope is very important to happiness. The Good Life is a life of brokenness and joy, of love and loss, all empowered by sure hope.

○○○○

The more personal dilemma of hope is what has been called the "*eudaimonia* gap." *Eudaimonia*, as we discussed earlier, is the Greek way of talking about human flourishing and happiness. But there is a problem. Our experiential reality is that we long for happiness yet can never fully attain and maintain it. Even with the best practices of physical and mental health, all of our happiness gets tainted and marred and never lasts. For many people, it is wrecked by poverty, disease, violence, injustice, and brokenness. And for all people, sooner or later, this flourishing life comes to an end. As the Christian scholar David Elliot points out, "The ills which limit happiness in these ways constitute a depressing gap between the kind of happiness we want and the kind we can reliably get." Most people, Christian or not, respond to this "*eudaimonia* gap" with melancholy resignation.[12] Many self-medicate to avoid the existential crisis of the gap.

This is where the Christian philosophy of hope is critical. The Christian hope is that God is going to return to restore the world to right, to bring light into darkness, to create a new creation of shalom and peace, to be present face-to-face with his creatures. It is this hope alone that can bridge the *eudaimonia* gap between our experience now and our deepest longings. Christian hope for the coming age of flourishing is not escapism but the means by which our otherwise demoralized emotions and our actions are buoyed and energized. As the Christian philosopher David Naugle cleverly observes, biblical happiness is "edenistic," not "hedonistic"—it is based on God's creation and re-creation of the world.[13]

This Christian hope is more than baptized optimism. It is not just the natural inclination of certain personality types. Hope is a virtue to be cultivated. Hope is a virtue of the will that can teach us to embrace both hardships and joys, because it is more than a mere emotion. Even in the midst of the darkest trials, Christians can still have hope. Mysteriously, it is in the darkest times that hope shines the brightest. This was the experience of the ancient prophets, the apostles, and innumerable believers down through history.

○○○○

Among today's many psychological therapeutic techniques, one that is particularly promising is called positive psychology. Positive psychology emphasizes habits that people can develop to live more flourishing lives. Several of the theorists within positive psychology have realized that this requires more than just techniques; it also requires a vision for a better future. In short, these secular psychologists realize that for people to flourish, they need hope.

As a result, one subbranch of positive psychology is called hope therapy. Hope, according to psychologist C. Richard Snyder, consists of two main components—the ability to plan pathways to our desired goals and the motivation and ability to use these pathways.[14] Therapists have found that people without this kind of hope rarely get better or learn to find balanced lives worth living. Humans can't survive without some kind of hope.

Roberto Benigni's character Guido in *Life Is Beautiful* knew this when he and his son were taken to a concentration camp. At great risk to his life, Guido playfully acted like the camp they were in was actually an elaborate game where the winning team won their own tank at the end. This kept the innocent young Giosué from losing hope—a hope that kept him alive until he was reunited with his mother when the camp was liberated.

But today hope is hard to find, especially when the nihilistic air we breathe is regularly pumped in by high-powered fans of skepticism and apathy. Additionally, even if we learn techniques of short-term goal setting, these will not be enough to sustain us through our complex lives, especially when we experience great suffering and tragedy. A friend of mine is the corporate chaplain for a large regional chain of fast-food restaurants, and he reports that not a day goes by when some employee—from fry-makers to upper management—breaks down in hopelessness because of some personal crisis. This is despite living in the most prosperous country in the world. Even advanced "hope therapy" is insufficient to satisfy the human soul's need for transcendence, for something that goes beyond the grave and this fallen world as we know it.

The English theoretical physicist and Anglican priest Sir John Polkinghorne observes that we need some kind of "moral cosmology" or else we won't have the emotional capital for the costly demands of caring for an aging parent or handicapped child. Hope in a real future—an embodied life after death—alone "is the foundation of a moral view that supports and enables the costly demands of fidelity and duty."[15] This is because "hope can sustain the acceptance of such limitation by delivering us from *the tyranny of the present*, the feeling of need to grab as much as we can before all opportunity passes away forever. We are enabled to live our lives not in the spirit of *carpe diem* but *sub specie aeternitatis* (in the light of eternity)."[16]

Most of the world today does not have this kind of future hope. But the Christian philosophy emphasizes precisely this—an honest assessment of the brokenness of life that is always oriented toward a sure hope for God's restoration of true flourishing to the world. This is the Good Life according to the Christian philosophy.

○ ○ ○ ○

We began our discussion by looking at the walls of the ancient church of Dura-Europos. As we discovered, Christians used to think of Jesus as the Great Philosopher, but somehow this got lost. I suggested that the loss of Christianity as a whole-life philosophy has saddled us with four problems:

1. Our Christian faith is often *disconnected* from other aspects of our human lives. Christianity has become merely a religion rather than a philosophy of life.

2. We naturally look to other sources—*alternative gurus*—to give us the wisdom needed to live flourishing lives, to find the Good Life.

3. We have stopped asking a *set of big questions* that Holy Scripture is seeking to answer—questions about how the world really works and how to live in it.

4. We have *limited our witness* to the world.

On the greatest of the philosophical questions—how to live a whole, meaningful, and flourishing life—modern Christianity clearly suffers from these four problems. Even though Jesus said that he is "the way and the truth and the life" (John 14:6) and that he has come to give us "life to the full" (John 10:10), the experience of most Christians today is that our faith is religious but not philosophical.

Here's a quick test of that. In the two verses that I just quoted from the Gospel of John, what do you think "life" refers to? If your answer is "salvation" or "heaven" or something comparable, then you've just proven my point.

Herein lies the nuanced complication. Those future, heavenly-salvation glosses for "life" are not wrong. They're just incomplete. That vertical and religious interpretation of "life" is part of the story but not the whole. It's the conclusion to the book but it's not the whole narrative.

This is why the fastest-growing religion in the world is a dark perversion of Christianity—what is called the health-and-wealth gospel. These pyramid-scheme false teachers are half right, and that's precisely why they are so effective and so dangerous. They are perceiving, affirming, and providing an answer to the great human question, How do I find a whole, meaningful, and flourishing life *now*? The half of their ministry that is correct is the recognition that Christianity is indeed speaking to this great question. But the dark, perverted, and ultimately deadly half of their teaching is a failure to recognize that a flourishing life, according to Jesus, includes suffering, disappointment, and loss.

The Christian musician Sara Groves wrote the poignant song "This House" about returning to her childhood home as her parents prepared to sell the house.[17] As she reflects on the good and the brokenness of her upbringing, she summarizes it with four terse and effective words—sad, fruitful, broken, true. What a beautiful description of the flourishing reality of the Christian philosophy! True happiness is found in the way of Jesus, and that flourishing life is a complex cocktail that must be drunk in its fullness to feel its effect—sad, fruitful, broken, true.

The reality is that Jesus means it when he says that he has come to bring people abundant life. This includes life now, not just an ethereal future. That flourishing life begins the moment anyone becomes a part of Jesus through faith and hope in him. But our happiness is not complete, and life is mysteriously found in the midst of pain and loss, not in everything getting better and better. Life and happiness are found, not by searching out the perfect Instagram photo that we can tag with #blessed, but in learning to embrace the fullness of life's emotions and circumstances—dark and bright—through the virtue of hope.

When we return to Holy Scripture, looking to Jesus as the faithful guru of true happiness, we find the biblical answers to be sophisticated, profound, and life-transforming wisdom. When we, as the church, look to Jesus as our Lord, Savior, King, Priest, and Philosopher, we come to know what it means to be a Christian. We learn what it means to take on our role as ministers of the good news. We will be salt and light whose well-lived lives glorify God and draw people to him (Matt. 5:13–16) as we "shine among them like stars in the sky as [we] hold firmly to the word of [the Good] Life" (Phil. 2:15–16).

Notes

Philosophers, Martyrs, and Canoes

1. The history of this ancient fortress city is fascinating, including what we can learn about early Christianity from it. For a general introduction from Yale University with pictures and graphics, see http://media.artgallery.yale.edu/dura europos/dura.html. On the house church, one recent study is Michael Peppard, *The World's Oldest Church: Bible, Art, and Ritual at Dura-Europos, Syria* (New Haven: Yale University Press, 2016), though some of Peppard's conclusions about early Christianity are unsubstantiated. Thanks to Robert S. Kinney for first making this connection for me in *Hellenistic Dimensions of the Gospel of Matthew: Background and Rhetoric*, Wissenschaftliche Untersuchungen zum Neuen Testament 2/414 (Tübingen: Mohr Siebeck, 2016).

2. C. Kavin Rowe, *One True Life: The Stoics and Early Christians as Rival Traditions* (New Haven: Yale University Press, 2016), 171.

3. Peter J. Leithart, *The Theopolitan Vision* (West Monroe, LA: Theopolis Books, 2019), 9.

4. Nick Offerman, *Paddle Your Own Canoe: One Man's Fundamentals for Delicious Living* (New York: Dutton, 2013).

5. See, for example, Jack Jenkins, "'Nones' Now as Big as Evangelicals, Catholics in the US," *Religion News Service*, https://religionnews.com/2019/03/21/non es-now-as-big-as-evangelicals-catholics-in-the-us/.

The Genius of Ancient Philosophy

1. I would like to thank various schools and people who helped me explore these ideas at various stages of their development, including Todd Billings and Kristen Deede Johnson, who invited me for lectures at Western Seminary, and Robert Yarbrough, who invited me to deliver the Bantam Lectures at Covenant Seminary.

2. Steve Martin, *A Wild and Crazy Guy*, Warner Brothers Records, 1978.

3. This line comes from his routine *A Wild and Crazy Guy*. For more on Martin's own journey, see the delightful autobiography of his early life, *Born Standing Up* (New York: Scribner, 2007), in which the themes of philosophy and comedy are interwoven.

4. There is comparable wisdom to be found in the Asian traditions of Buddhism, Hinduism, and Confucianism. My focus on Greek philosophy here is largely because of my greater familiarity with it and because of the more direct interaction between this tradition and that of the Bible and early Christianity. But the overall point I am making about Greek and Roman philosophy is patently true of the Eastern traditions as well—they are teaching a way of life that promises happiness.

5. *What Is Ancient Philosophy?* is the title of one of the most important books on Greek philosophy in the twentieth century, written by Pierre Hadot. Hadot shows that ancient philosophy was a way of life. The English translation of the 1995 French edition is *What Is Ancient Philosophy?*, trans. Michael Chase (Cambridge, MA: Belknap, 2004).

6. One of the oldest and leading academic journals that explores ancient Greek and Roman thought is appropriately called *Phronesis*.

7. See the summary report from the US Centers for Disease Control and Prevention at https://www.cdc.gov/vitalsigns/suicide/index.html.

8. See Stephen Pinker, *Enlightenment Now: The Case for Reason, Science, Humanism, and Progress* (New York: Penguin, 2019).

9. Darius Karłowicz, *Socrates and Other Saints: Early Christian Understandings of Reason and Philosophy*, trans. Artur Sebastian Rosman (Eugene, OR: Cascade, 2017), 66.

10. Hadot, *What Is Ancient Philosophy?*, 153. See also his book *Philosophy as a Way of Life: Spiritual Exercises from Socrates to Foucault*, trans. Michael Chase (Malden, MA: Blackwell, 1995).

11. Hadot, *What Is Ancient Philosophy?*, 56.

12. Quoted in Hadot, *What Is Ancient Philosophy?*, 56–57.

13. Aristotle, *Nicomachean Ethics* 1.1, trans. W. D. Ross, Internet Classics Archive, accessed March 10, 2020, http://classics.mit.edu/Aristotle/nicomachaen.1.i.html.

14. This is the image from one of the most famous passages from ancient philosophy: the cave scene from book seven of Plato's *Republic*.

15. From Dante's *The Divine Comedy*. This translation of the Latin is from Erich Auerbach, *Dante: Poet of the Secular World*, trans. Ralph Manheim (New York: New York Review Books, 2007), 151.

16. This is the description used by Hadot to describe Greek philosophy. He unpacks "spiritual exercises" to mean "practices which could be physical, as in dietary regimes, or discursive, as in dialogue and meditation, or intuitive, as in contemplation, but which were all intended to effect a modification and a transformation in the subject who practiced them." *What Is Ancient Philosophy?*, 6.

17. Kant, *Lectures on the Philosophical Encyclopedia*, quoted in Hadot, *What Is Ancient Philosophy?*, xiii.

18. Henry David Thoreau, *Walden* (New York: Thomas Y. Crowell, 1910), 17.

19. *The Good Place*, season 1, episode 1, "Pilot," aired September 19, 2016, on NBC.

The Philosophical "Big Ideas" in the Old Testament

1. A readable and informative description of Moses in synagogue art, including at Dura-Europos, can be found in Géza G. Xeravits, "The Figure of Moses in Ancient Synagogue Art," in *Mosebilder: Gedanken zur Rezeption einer literarischen Figur im Frühjudentum, frühen Christentum und der römisch-hellenistischen Literatur*, ed. Michael Sommer et al., Wissenschaftliche Untersuchungen zum Neuen Testament 390 (Tübingen: Mohr Siebeck, 2017), 415–28, accessible on the author's page at www.academia.edu.

2. Yoram Hazony, *The Philosophy of Hebrew Scripture* (Cambridge: Cambridge University Press, 2012).

3. Hazony, *Philosophy*, 12.

4. Hazony, *Philosophy*, 4.

5. Much of this discussion on knowing in Scripture is informed by several works by Dru Johnson, including *Scripture's Knowing: A Companion to Biblical Epistemology* (Eugene, OR: Wipf & Stock, 2015); *Biblical Knowing: A Scriptural Epistemology of Error* (Cambridge: James Clarke, 2013); and *Knowledge by Ritual: A Biblical Prolegomenon to Sacramental Theology* (Winona Lake, IN: Eisenbrauns, 2016).

6. Hazony suggests that the central theme of Jeremiah is "the question of how it is possible for the individual to distinguish truth from falsity and right from wrong in the face of the wildly contradictory views being promoted by prophets, priests, and political leaders" (*Philosophy*, 24–25). Jeremiah's reflections "constitute an early and substantively interesting attempt to develop a theory of knowledge" (*Philosophy*, 25).

7. For a more detailed exposition of this idea, see Gregory Vall, "An Epistemology of Faith: The Knowledge of God in Israel's Prophetic Literature," in Mary Healy and Robin A. Parry, eds., *The Bible and Epistemology* (Milton Keynes: Paternoster, 2007), 30–36. My comments here are largely dependent on this insightful discussion.

8. Much more could be said on this point, including the observation that the central theme of spiritual harlotry or adultery in Hosea can also be connected with this emphasis on knowledge, via the understanding that "knowing" is already integrated with (sexual) intimacy from Gen. 4:1 on.

9. The phrase "the fear of the LORD" is very important and appears fourteen times in Proverbs, not only as the conclusion to the prologue to the book (1:1–7) but also at other important junctures in the book such as 9:10 and 31:30. See the helpful discussion in Ryan P. O'Dowd, "A Chord of Three Strands: Epistemology in Job, Proverbs and Ecclesiastes," in Healy and Parry, *The Bible and Epistemology*, 67–68.

10. Raymond C. Van Leeuwen, "Wisdom Literature," in Kevin J. Vanhoozer, Craig G. Bartholomew, Daniel J. Treier, and N. T. Wright, eds., *Dictionary for*

Theological Interpretation of the Bible (Grand Rapids: Baker Academic, 2005), 849.

11. Garrett DeWeese has a succinct discussion of how Proverbs, Job, and Ecclesiastes function in these ways in his book *Doing Philosophy as a Christian* (Downers Grove, IL: InterVarsity, 2011), 55.

12. Hazony, *Philosophy*, 24.

13. Hazony, *Philosophy*, 59.

14. Hazony, *Philosophy*, 61.

15. Hazony, *Philosophy*, 61. For a helpful chart of the structure of the books of the Hebrew Bible, see Hazony, *Philosophy*, 35.

16. The quote and ideas here are from Hazony, *Philosophy*, 63. While I find Hazony's arguments about the Hebrew Scriptures convincing, he regularly misunderstands and misrepresents Christianity as if it distorts this vision. Quite the contrary, the New Testament sees itself as the fulfillment of this same goal and vision of being a blessing to all nations (thus fulfilling the promise to Abraham) through the coming of God's own Son, Jesus the Christ.

17. Hazony, *Philosophy*, 23.

18. Gary W. Moon, *Becoming Dallas Willard: The Formation of a Philosopher, Teacher, and Christ Follower* (Downers Grove, IL: IVP Books, 2018), 83.

19. Moon, *Becoming Dallas Willard*, 83.

The Philosophical "Big Ideas" in the New Testament

1. This re-creation can be found here: https://www.popularmechanics.com /science/health/a234/1282186/.

2. Joan Taylor, *What Did Jesus Look Like?* (London: Bloomsbury T&T Clark, 2018), 123–24.

3. Taylor, *What Did Jesus Look Like?*, 132.

4. Taylor, *What Did Jesus Look Like?*, 136.

5. J. R. R. Tolkien, *The Return of the King: Being the Third Part of the Lord of the Rings* (New York: Ballantine Books, 1965), 166.

6. Seneca, Letter 108, in *Selected Letters*, trans. Elaine Fantham (Oxford: Oxford University Press, 2010), 24.

7. Dallas Willard has explored Jesus's intellectual prowess in his essay "Jesus the Logician," which can be found in his book, *The Great Omission: Reclaiming Jesus's Essential Teachings on Discipleship* (San Francisco: HarperCollins, 2006).

8. We have long called these nine macarisms the "Beatitudes" because of the Latin word that is used to translate Matthew's Greek text, *beatus* (pronounced "be-a-toos"). Both Matthew's Greek word *makarios* and the Latin translation *beatus* were used when a philosopher would pronounce to his disciples the way to find true happiness. *Makarios* was used alongside *eudaimonia* in Greek philosophy as vision casting for how to live well.

9. Robert Kinney, *Hellenistic Dimensions of the Gospel of Matthew* (Tübingen: Mohr Siebeck, 2016), 215.

10. Framing humanity's sin problem as a matter of worship or love is a deeply Augustinian tradition. Helpful resources to explore this more include James K. A.

Smith, *You Are What You Love: The Spiritual Power of Habit* (Grand Rapids: Brazos, 2016), and David K. Naugle, *Reordered Love, Reordered Lives: Learning the Deep Meaning of Happiness* (Grand Rapids: Eerdmans, 2008).

A Big Emotional Debate

1. George Saunders, "Escape from Spiderhead," *New Yorker*, December 13, 2010, https://www.newyorker.com/magazine/2010/12/20/escape-from-spiderhead. The story also appears in his collection *Tenth of December: Stories* (New York: Random House, 2013).

2. *Oxford English Dictionary*, 2nd ed. (2004), s.v. "emotion."

3. Kevin Vanhoozer, *Remythologizing Theology* (New York: Cambridge University Press, 2010), 404–5.

4. Vanhoozer, *Remythologizing*, 404.

5. Martha Nussbaum, *The Therapy of Desire: Theory and Practice in Hellenistic Ethics* (Princeton: Princeton University Press, 1994).

6. This discussion and throughout the rest of the chapter has been greatly helped by Matthew Elliott's *Faithful Feelings: Rethinking Emotion in the New Testament* (Grand Rapids: Kregel, 2006).

7. Plato, *Phaedrus* 246b.

8. Elliott, *Faithful Feelings*, 60.

9. Descartes's *The Passions of the Soul*, completed in 1649, reflects the new scientific and materialistic view of the world that quickly came to dominate European understanding.

10. Elliott, *Faithful Feelings*, 23.

11. Marc Alan Schelske, *The Wisdom of Your Heart: Discovering the God-Given Purpose and Power of Your Emotions* (Colorado Springs: David C. Cook, 2017), 25–26.

12. This discussion is informed by Elliott, *Faithful Feelings*, 66–69.

13. Elliott, *Faithful Feelings*, 63.

14. Nussbaum, *Therapy*, 78.

15. Ludwig Edelstein, *The Meaning of Stoicism* (Cambridge, MA: Harvard University Press, 1966), 2, quoted in Elliott, *Faithful Feelings*, 76.

16. Elliott, *Faithful Feelings*, 76–77.

17. Nussbaum, *Therapy*, 96–97.

18. Elliott, *Faithful Feelings*, 52. The following account is based on Schelske's discussion of Damasio in *Wisdom of Your Heart*, 125–28.

19. Antonio R. Damasio, *Descartes' Error: Emotion, Reason and the Human Brain* (New York: Harper Perennial, 1995), 34–51, esp. 46–51.

20. Damasio, *Descartes' Error*, 51. After exploring the many possibilities of why Elliot was unable to make decisions, Dr. Damasio concludes, "I was certain that in Elliot the defect was accompanied by a reduction in emotional reactivity and feeling" (51).

21. Elizabeth Johnston and Leah Olson, *The Feeling Brain: The Biology and Psychology of Emotions* (New York: Norton, 2015), 308–9.

22. Elliott, *Faithful Feelings*, 54.

Christianity's Sophisticated Solution

1. I cannot provide a comprehensive list of the emotions attributed to God in the Old Testament, but here are some representative examples: loving (Jer. 31:3; cf. John 3:16; 1 John 4:8); being angry (Deut. 9:22; Ps. 7:11; cf. Rom. 1:18); grieving (Gen. 6:6; Ps. 78:40); being jealous (Exod. 20:5; 34:14; Josh. 24:19); having compassion (Deut. 32:36; Judg. 2:18; Ps. 135:14).

2. For a great discussion of the history and theology of impassibility, see Kevin Vanhoozer, *Remythologizing Theology* (New York: Cambridge University Press, 2010), 387–433.

3. Marc Alan Schelske, *The Wisdom of Your Heart: Discovering the God-Given Purpose and Power of Your Emotions* (Colorado Springs: David C. Cook, 2017), 120.

4. John Calvin, *Commentarius in Harmoniam Evangelicarum,* comments on Matthew 26:37, quoted in B. B. Warfield, "On the Emotional Life of Our Lord," in *The Person and Work of Christ* (Phillipsburg, NJ: P&R, 1989), 93.

5. Warfield, "Emotional Life," 93.

6. Warfield, "Emotional Life," 139.

7. Warfield, "Emotional Life," 141.

8. Bill Bright, *Have You Made the Wonderful Discovery of the Spirit-Filled Life* (1966; repr., Orlando: New Life Resources, 2005); for an online version, see https://www.cru.org/us/en/train-and-grow/spiritual-growth/the-spirit-filled-life.html.

9. Italics in Scripture quotations have been added for emphasis.

10. "What Is Stoicism? A Definition & 9 Stoic Exercises to Get You Started," Daily Stoic, https://dailystoic.com/what-is-stoicism-a-definition-3-stoic-exercises-to-get-you-started/.

11. This translation comes from my *The Sermon on the Mount and Human Flourishing: A Theological Commentary* (Grand Rapids: Baker Academic, 2018), 217–18.

The Necessity of Relationships

1. Wallace Stegner, *Crossing to Safety* (New York: Random House, Modern Library, 2002), back cover.

2. From the publisher's description for the 2007 Random House edition.

3. Stegner, *Crossing to Safety*, 96.

4. Terry Tempest Williams, introduction to Stegner, *Crossing to Safety*, xvi.

5. Roy F. Baumeister and Mark R. Leary, "The Need to Belong: Desire for Interpersonal Attachments as a Fundamental Human Motivation," *Psychological Bulletin* 117.3 (1995): 497–529.

6. Baumeister and Leary, "The Need to Belong," 497.

7. The best translation of the *Moralia* is found in 15 volumes of the Loeb Classical Library. The "Advice to Bride and Groom" is in *Moralia*, vol. 2, trans. Frank Cole Babbitt, Loeb Classical Library 222 (Cambridge, MA: Harvard University Press, 1928), 299.

8. Elizabeth Brake, "Marriage and Domestic Partnership," in *Stanford Encyclopedia of Philosophy*, ed. Edward N. Zalta, winter 2016 ed., https://plato.stanford.edu/entries/marriage/.

9. Cicero, *On Duties*, ed. M. T. Griffin and E. M. Atkins (Cambridge: Cambridge University Press, 1991), 1.53–55, pp. 22–23.

10. According to the Commonwealth of Massachusetts website: https://www.mass.gov/service-details/why-is-massachusetts-a-commonwealth.

11. Anne Rooney, *How the World Works: Philosophy from the Ancient Greeks to Great Thinkers of Modern Times* (London: Sirius, 2019), 162.

12. Rooney's discussion of Plato and Aristotle is succinct and helpful. See *How the World Works*, 163–66.

13. Fred Miller, "Aristotle's Political Theory," *Stanford Encyclopedia of Philosophy*, ed. Edward N. Zalta, winter 2017 ed., https://plato.stanford.edu/entries/aristotle-politics/.

14. Miller, "Aristotle's Political Theory."

15. Rooney, *How the World Works*, 164–65.

16. Miller, "Aristotle's Political Theory."

17. Lauren Faust, "My Little NON-Homophobic, NON-Racist, NON-Smart-Shaming Pony: A Rebuttal," *Ms.*, December 24, 2010, https://msmagazine.com/2010/12/24/my-little-non-homophobic-non-racist-non-smart-shaming-pony-a-rebuttal/.

18. J. R. R. Tolkien, "On Fairy-Stories," in *The Tolkien Reader* (New York: Ballantine Books, 1966), 34.

19. *Vatican Saying* 52; translation and discussion from John M. Rist, "Epicurus on Friendship," *Classical Philology* 75, no. 2 (1980): 122.

20. As quoted and discussed in Alain de Botton, *The Consolations of Philosophy* (New York: Penguin, 2001), 57.

21. One particularly helpful and readable discussion of Aristotle on friendship is chapters 1 and 2 of Kevin Vost's *The Four Friendships: From Aristotle to Aquinas* (New York: Angelico Press, 2018).

22. Michael Pakaluk, *Other Selves: Philosophers on Friendship* (Indianapolis: Hackett, 1991), xi.

23. Diogenes Laertius, *Lives of Eminent Philosophers* 5.31, in *Lives of Eminent Philosophers: Books 1–5*, trans. R. D. Hicks, Loeb Classical Library 184 (Cambridge, MA: Harvard University Press, 1925), 478–79. Craig Keener has an excellent discussion in *The Gospel of John: A Commentary* (Grand Rapids: Baker Academic, 2012), 2:1004–13.

24. This is the title of the 2018 translation by Professor Philip Freeman: *How to Be a Friend: An Ancient Guide to True Friendship* (Princeton: Princeton University Press, 2018).

25. Philip Freeman, "How to Be a Good Friend, according to an Ancient Philosopher," *Time*, October 9, 2018.

26. See "Friends Like These: On Thoreau and Emerson," Daegan Miller's *Los Angeles Review of Books* review of Jeffrey S. Cramer's *Solid Seasons: The Friendship of Henry David Thoreau and Ralph Waldo Emerson*. https://lareviewofbooks.org/article/friends-like-these-on-thoreau-and-emerson/.

27. Pakaluk, *Other Selves*, x.

28. Wesley Hill, *Spiritual Friendship: Finding Love in the Church as a Celibate Gay Christian* (Grand Rapids: Brazos, 2015), 6–7.

29. Niobe Way, *Deep Secrets: Boys, Friendships, and the Crisis of Connection* (Cambridge, MA: Harvard University Press, 2013), discussed in Hill, *Spiritual Friendship*, 8–9.

30. Hill, *Spiritual Friendship*, 7.

31. Aimee Byrd, *Why Can't We Be Friends? Avoidance Is Not Purity* (Phillipsburg, NJ: P&R, 2018). Thanks to Anna Poole Mondal for this helpful resource and summary.

32. Hill, *Spiritual Friendship*, 15–16.

33. Craig A. Williams, *Reading Roman Friendship* (Cambridge: Cambridge University Press, 2012), 17, quoted in Hill, *Spiritual Friendship*, 16n4.

Christianity's Renewed Relationships

1. For more discussion of how Matthew treats family and how this relates to soul care and therapy, see my article "Christian Psychology and the Gospel of Matthew," *Edification: The Journal of the Society of Christian Psychology* 3, no. 2 (2009): 39–48.

2. Augustine, *The City of God*, trans. Marcus Dods (Altenmünster, Germany: Jazzybee Verlag, 2015).

3. Peter J. Leithart, *The Theopolitan Vision* (n.p.: Theopolis Books, 2019), xiii.

4. This paragraph follows Leithart, *Theopolitan Vision*, 14.

5. Leithart, *Theopolitan Vision*, 15–17.

6. Leithart, *Theopolitan Vision*, 11.

7. This paragraph is based on the helpful articulation of Jack Franicevich in his essay, "On Friendship," posted at https://theopolisinstitute.com/on-friendship/, August 20, 2019. The quote from Hugh Black is found there as well.

8. Scholars regularly emphasize the kinship relationship between Ruth and Naomi, but I think it is helpful to recognize their relationship as also being an example of faithful friendship.

9. Plutarch called *parrēsia* the "language of friendship." For a more thorough exploration of the term and its context, see Clarence E. Glad, *Paul and Philodemus: Adaptability in Epicurean and Early Christian Psychagogy*, Supplements to Novum Testamentum 81 (Leiden: Brill, 1995), 104–6. Thanks to Cody King for this reference.

10. Seneca, Letter 3, "On True and False Friendship," in *Letters from a Stoic*, vol. 1, trans. Richard Mott Gummere, reprinted in *Seneca Six Pack: Six Essential Texts* (Los Angeles: Enhanced Media, 2016), 31.

Humans, We Have a Problem

1. There has been some debate over the centuries about this statement. The times when animals appear to commit suicide is best explained as the result of severe changes that create aberrant behavior, not the psychological state that leads

a person to imagine their own death. A well-researched article on this is Melissa Hogenboom, "Many Animals Seem to Kill Themselves, but It Is Not Suicide," BBC, July 6, 2016, http://www.bbc.com/earth/story/20160705-many-animals -seem-to-kill-themselves-but-it-is-not-suicide.

2. *Deadpool*, directed by Tim Miller (Los Angeles: Twentieth Century Fox Home Entertainment, 2016).

3. Augustine, *The City of God*, trans. Marcus Dods (Altenmünster, Germany: Jazzybee Verlag, 2015), 211.

4. Darrin McMahon, *Happiness: A History* (New York: Atlantic Monthly Press, 2007), 3.

5. Augustine, *The City of God*, 211.

6. For an insightful critique of the limited metaphysical vision of Harari, see Roger Scruton, "The Turing Machine Speaks: Silicon Valley Guru Yuval Noah Harari's Chilling Post-Humanism," *City Journal* (Summer 2019), https://www .city-journal.org/yuval-noah-harari.

7. Harari, *Sapiens: A Brief History of Humankind* (New York: HarperCollins, 2015), 376.

8. Harari, *Sapiens*, 391.

9. Harari, *Sapiens*, 391.

10. Hubert Dreyfus and Sean Dorrance Kelly, *All Things Shining: Reading the Western Classics to Find Meaning in a Secular Age* (New York: Free Press, 2011), xi.

11. John M. Grohol, "Mental Health Professionals: US Statistics 2017," *World of Psychology* (blog), PsychCentral, April 9, 2019, https://psychcentral.com/blog /mental-health-professionals-us-statistics-2017/; Matthew Jones, "11 Billion Reasons the Self Help Industry Doesn't Want You to Know the Truth about Happiness," *Inc.*, October 19, 2017, https://www.inc.com/matthew-jones/11-billion -reasons-self-help-industry-doesnt-want-you-to-know-truth-about-happiness .html; Lindsay Myers, "The Self-Help Industry Helps Itself to Billions of Dollars," BrainBlogger, May 23, 2014, https://brainblogger.com/2014/05/23/the-self-help -industry-helps-itself-to-billions-of-dollars/.

12. This comes from Jeff Guin's biography, *Manson: The Life and Times of Charles Manson* (New York: Simon & Schuster, 2014).

13. Alain de Botton and John Armstrong, *Art as Therapy* (London: Phaidon, 2013), 64.

14. De Botton and Armstrong, *Art as Therapy*, 5.

15. "The School of Life: What We Believe," The School of Life, accessed March 11, 2020, https://www.theschooloflife.com/thebookoflife/tsol-what-we-believe/.

16. This is from the description of the seminar "Finding Meaning without Religion," taught by Pierz Newton-John at the Melbourne, Australia, branch of the School of Life, https://www.theschooloflife.com/melbourne/events/work shops/finding-meaning-without-religion/.

17. Alain de Botton, *Religion for Atheists: A Non-Believer's Guide to the Uses of Religion* (New York: Vintage, 2012), 11–13.

18. *Hector and the Search for Happiness*, directed by Peter Chelsom (Los Angeles: Twentieth Century Fox Home Entertainment, 2014).

19. Unsigned review of *Hector and the Search for Happiness*, by François Lelord, trans. Lorenza Garcia, *Publisher's Weekly*, accessed March 23, 2019, https://www.publishersweekly.com/978-0-14-311839-8.

Christianity's Whole, Meaningful, and Flourishing Life

1. Justin, *Second Apology* 8.13. Ante-Nicene Christian Library: Translations of the Writings of the Fathers down to A.D. 325, vol. 2, ed. Alexander Roberts and James Donaldson (Edinburgh: T&T Clark, 1867), 83.

2. Fyodor Dostoevsky, *The Karamozov Brothers*, trans. Ignat Avsey (Oxford: Oxford University Press, 1994), 69.

3. Augustine, *City of God* 19.1, in *The City of God, Books XVII–XXII*, trans. Gerald G. Walsh and Daniel J. Honan, The Fathers of the Church 24 (Washington, DC: Catholic University of America Press, 2010), 187.

4. Darius Karłowicz, *Socrates and Other Saints: Early Christian Understandings of Reason and Philosophy*, trans. Artur Sebastian Rosman (Eugene, OR: Cascade, 2017), 48.

5. For an excellent scholarly treatment of the theme of happiness throughout the Bible, see Brent Strawn, ed., *The Bible and the Pursuit of Happiness: What the Old and New Testaments Teach Us about the Good Life* (Oxford: Oxford University Press, 2012).

6. For further exploration of the Beatitudes, the translation of happy/flourishing, and connection with Psalm 1, see my *The Sermon on the Mount and Human Flourishing: A Theological Commentary* (Grand Rapids: Baker Academic, 2018).

7. True happiness depends on right knowing, and right knowing depends on trusting the right authorities. See Dru Johnson, *Scripture's Knowing: A Companion to Biblical Epistemology* (Eugene, OR: Wipf & Stock, 2015), 16.

8. C. S. Lewis, *The Weight of Glory and Other Addresses* (Grand Rapids: Eerdmans, 1965), 1–2. Piper's discussion can be found in John Piper, *Desiring God*, rev. ed. (Colorado Springs: Multnomah, 2011), 19–20.

9. C. S. Lewis, *The Screwtape Letters* (New York: HarperCollins, 2001), 65.

10. Irenaeus, *Against Heresies* (n.p.: Aeterna Press, 2016), 372.

11. Richard Bauckham and Trevor Hart, *Hope against Hope: Christian Eschatology in Contemporary Context* (London: Darton, Longman & Todd, 1999), 83.

12. David Elliot, *Hope and Christian Ethics* (New York: Cambridge University Press, 2017), 5.

13. David K. Naugle, *Reordered Love, Reordered Lives: Learning the Deep Meaning of Happiness* (Grand Rapids: Eerdmans, 2008), 13–17.

14. C. Richard Snyder, *Handbook of Hope: Theory, Measures, and Applications* (San Diego: Academic Press, 2000).

15. John Polkinghorne, *The God of Hope and the End of the World* (New Haven: Yale University Press, 2003), 48.

16. Polkinghorne, *The God of Hope*, 48–49.

17. Sara Groves, "This House," track 6 on *Fireflies and Songs*, Integrity Music, 2009.